Wedding Cakes

A · WILTON · ALBUM

Credits

Creative Director	Richard Tracy
Copy Director	Marie DeBenedicitis
Copywriter	Linda Skender
Senior Decorator	Amy Rohr
Cake Decorators	Mary Gavenda
	Corky Kagay
	Susan Matusiak
Photographer	Kathy Sanders
Photo Assistant	Christy Gozdik
Production Coordinator	Mary Stahulak
Production	RNB Graphics

For complete information on Wilton products, see the current
Wilton Yearbook of Cake Decorating. Many products shown will be
available at your local Wilton dealer. You can also write or call:
Wilton Enterprises, Inc.
Caller Service 1604
2240 W. 75th St.
Woodridge, IL 60517
1-312-963-7100

For photography purposes, designs were decorated with royal icing.

Library of Congress Catalog Card Number: 88-51509
Printed in U.S.A.

Wedding cakes are very special. Since the tradition of the wedding cake began thousands of years ago, it has symbolized good luck, fertility and a long, happy life together for the bride and groom.

Today, a bride considers the wedding cake a very important and precious part of her wedding. It is the focal point of the reception and one of the final remembrances the bridal couple has of their happy wedding day. In fact, traditionally, the top tier of the wedding cake is saved for the bride and groom to serve when they return from their honeymoon or on their first wedding anniversary.

Brides choose their wedding cakes with care, often desiring to match their wedding theme and bridal party colors. Contemporary, country, traditional, and Victorian are the most popular wedding themes. On a wedding cake the theme can be carried out by the use of flowers, hearts, birds, bells, swans, angels, doves, lace, ribbons, ruffles and garlands. If a cake has flowers, the season of the year may determine the type and color; flowers may also be tinted to match the bridal party colors, which may coincide with the seasonal colors.

Wilton has been pleasing brides with wedding cake designs for over half a century. The magnificent designs in this book continue that wonderful Wilton tradition. Among this inspiring collection are cakes from classic simplicity to elaborate embellishment, including an unforgettable selection featuring the Australian, Lambeth, and Philippine methods of decorating, rolled fondant, and simply luscious Cheese Cake tiers.

Keep in mind that the designs shown can coordinate with the bride's color, flower and ornament preferences. Cake sizes can also be adapted to serve her guests.

Contents

Wedding Cakes
Up to 150 Servings
4

Wedding Cakes
Over 150 Servings
28

Shower and Anniversary Cakes
50

Baking, Decorating How-To's and Recipes
66

Patterns
78

*Romantic Monograms shown
(instructions follow)*

Romantic Monograms

Shown on preceding page.

*The color flow heart plaque personalizes this
towering heart and round combination. Sweet pea
borders look so distinctive and are easy to do.
Note that flowers at bases are piped
with only two petals.*

- 9 in. Heart Pans
- 16 in. Round Pans
- Decorating Tips 3, 4, 6, 104, 124
- 11 in. Heart Separator Plates
- 10¼ in. Roman Columns
- Pearl Leaf Puff
- Cake Dividing Set
- Cake Circles, Tuk 'n Ruffle,
- Fanci-Foil Wrap
- Dowel Rods
- Color Flow Mix
- Script Heart & Letters Patterns (see pattern index)

- Icing Color: Cornflower Blue
- Wedding Ornament: *Lacy Elegance*

With blue color flow icing, outline Heart Pattern with tip 3 and fill in. Let dry.

Ice and prepare 2-layer cakes for pillar construction. For drop strings: Dot mark sides of heart at 2½ in. intervals; using Cake Dividing Set, mark round cake sides into 16th. Connect dot marks with tip 4 double drop strings. Pipe tip 6 bead hearts at points.

Edge cake tops, plate and color flow heart with tip 104 and bases with tip 124 sweet peas. Using Script Letters Pattern as a guide, pipe tip 3 initials on heart plaque. Trim cake sides with tip 3 dots. Attach styrofoam to separator plate with royal icing to support color flow heart.

At reception, assemble tier on pillars. Attach color flow heart to styrofoam block with dots of royal icing. Add Pearl Leaf Puff and Lacy Elegance. *Serves 100 without top tier. If top cake is served, it will serve 124.*

Swirling Grace

*Dozens of pretty two-tone flowers gracefully flow
down the sides of classic round tiers.*

- Round Tier Set
- 14 in. Round Pans
- Decorating Tips 3, 14, 16, 21, 32, 45, 129, 225, 349
- Cake Circles
- Tuk 'n Ruffle, Fanci-Foil Wrap
- Cake Dividing Set
- Dowel Rods
- Icing Color: Cornflower Blue/Willow Green (blend together for teal shade)
- Wedding Ornament: *Natural Beauty*

Make drop flowers in two shades and sizes–60 light and 40 dark with tip 225; 85 light and 60 dark with tip 129. Add tip 3 dot centers.

Ice and prepare cakes for spiked pillar and stacked construction. Round Tier Set cakes may be torted; 14 in. is 2 layers deep. Using Cake Dividing Set, with toothpick, divide tiers, starting with top tier, into the following intervals: 8ths, 8ths, 12ths and 16ths.

Connect marks with 1½ in. deep garland markings. Also mark a guideline for ribbon 1½ in. from top on side of 2nd tier.

On top tier, pipe zigzag garlands and top shell border with tip 14. Edge remaining tops and all bases with tip 16 shell borders. Pipe tip 16 zigzag garlands and tip 32 columns on sides of stacked tiers. Add tip 45 ribbon and bow to side of 2nd tier.

Trim each tier with rosettes–tip 16 on top tier, tip 21 on the rest. Place Natural Beauty on cake, attach flowers to ornament, cake tops and sides. Trim with tip 349 leaves. *Serves 107.*

Darling

Elegant fondant-covered trio and flowing, glowing Kolor-Flo Fountain strike just the right note of drama and flair. Dainty ribbon bows highlight the exquisite precision of our Australian Method cake.

- Oval Pan Set (2 smallest size pans are used)
- 14 in. Round Pans
- Decorating Tips 2, 4, 362
- 8½ in. Oval Separator Plate (1 needed)
- 16 in. Round Separator Plates (2 needed)
- 9 in. Grecian Spiked Pillars, 13¾ in. Roman Columns
- Kolor-Flo Fountain
- Cake Circles
- Dowel Rods
- Stringwork Patterns A, B, C (see pattern index)
- Icing Color: Pink
- Wedding Ornament: *Happy Heart*
- Ribbon, silk roses and greenery

Cover 2-layer cakes with rolled fondant and prepare for stacked and spiked pillar construction.

Edge bases of cakes with tip 362 shell borders. With a pin, mark coordinating patterns on sides of tiers.

Note: All Australian Method "stringwork" is done with royal icing. When overpiping, pipe each new line and allow icing to dry so area doesn't shift or collapse from the weight.

Pipe tip 4 scalloped and straight extensions to serve as bases for curtaining. The extensions are made up of 6 lines on oval tiers; 8 lines on round cake. Each line is piped straight onto the previous line.

Paint curtaining areas pink (dilute a small amount of icing color in 1 ounce of kirsh). Let dry.

Pipe curtaining with tip 2. When thoroughly dry, trim extensions with tip 2 drop strings. Edge curtaining with tip 2 beads. Trim cake sides with tip 2 dots. Pipe tip 2 beads around spiked pillars. Attach ribbon bows with dots of icing.

At reception: Set up fountain, position tiers on pillars, arrange roses and greenery. Add Happy Heart.
Serves 107.

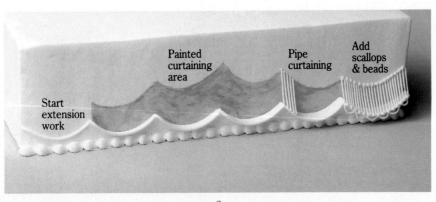

Start extension work

Painted curtaining area

Pipe curtaining

Add scallops & beads

Swan Symphony

*Graceful swans stand serenely as delicate strings
dance from shell to shell.*

- 6 in. Round Pans
- 11 x 15 in. Sheet Pans
- Decorating Tips 3, 14, 17, 32
- Serene Swans
- Swan Pillars
- 8 in. Separator Plates
- Cake Dividing Set
- Dowel Rods
- Cake Circle
- Cake base board 17½ x 21½ in. covered with white Fanci-Foil Wrap and trimmed with Tuk 'n Ruffle
- 12 x 16 in. rectangle cake board covered with foil and trimmed with ¾ in. wide satin ribbon
- Icing Color: Lemon Yellow
- Floral Puff Accents (5 needed)
- Wedding Ornament: *Splendid*

Prepare 2-layer cakes for pillar construction. Divide top tier into 8ths and connect marks with tip 14 e-motion garlands. Edge base with tip 32 upright shell border. Pipe tip 3 overlapping double drop strings. Trim with tip 14 stars. Edge cake top with tip 17 shell border.

Trim separator plate on top of sheet with tip 14 e-motion scrolls.

For border at top of sheet, mark 1½ in. intervals around cake edge. Pipe tip 32 upright shells. Trim with tip 3 triple drop strings. Add tip 14 stars. Using shells as your guide, pipe tip 14 e-motion garlands around cake top. Pipe tip 32 shell border at base. Trim with tip 3 drop strings and tip 14 stars.

At reception, place top tier on Swan Pillars. Add floral puff accents to swans and plate. Position swans and Splendid. *Serves 75.*

Flower Garlands

*Dainty lavender blooms and graceful filigree trims
have an engaging effect on classic round and
hexagon tiers.*

- 6 x 3 in. Round Pan
- 9, 12 in. Hexagon Pans
- 16 in. Round Pans
- Decorating Tips 3, 225, 349, 501, 502, 504
- 10 in. Hexagon Plates
- 5 in. Grecian Pillars, Snap-On Filigree
- Rosy Puff Accent (1 needed)
- Curved Triangles (12 needed)
- Swirls (6 needed)
- Cake Circles, Fanci-Foil, Tuk 'n Ruffle
- Dowel Rods
- Cake Dividing Set
- Icing Colors: Violet, Golden Yellow
- Wedding Ornament: *Garden Romance*

Make 750 tip 225 drop flowers with tip 3 dot centers.

Prepare one-layer top tier and the remaining 2-layer tiers for stacked and pillar construction.

Using Cake Dividing Set, with toothpick, mark top tier into 6ths, bottom tier into 12ths. Connect marks with tip 3 drop string guidelines.

Trim separator plate on top of 12 in. hexagon with tip 501 e-motion. Pipe tip 501 upright shells on sides at corners of hexagons. Edge cake tops and bases with shell borders; tip 501 on 6 in., 502 on hexagons and tip 504 on 16 in.

Push Swirls into sides of 16 in. round. To attach flowers and Curved Triangles to sides, squeeze icing onto areas with tip 3. Trim flowers with tip 349 leaves.

At reception, add Snap-On Filigree to pillars. Position tiers on pillars and add Garden Romance. *Serves 172.*

Groom's Choice

*A luscious tribute to his good taste.
Garlands and filigree cluster handsomely
complement the wedding cake.*

- 9, 12 in. Hexagon Pans
- Decorating Tips 3, 131, 352, 501, 502, 504
- Swirls (6 needed)
- Cake Boards, Fanci-Foil Wrap
- Dowel Rods
- Decorator's Brush

Make 60 tip 131 drop flowers with tip 3 centers. "Paint" six Swirls with thinned royal icing, let dry.

Ice 2-layer cakes smooth. Assemble tiers using stacked construction method. With toothpick, mark garlands (1½ in deep) on cake sides. Cover marks with tip 502 zigzags.

Pipe shell borders – tip 501 on corners, tip 502 on cake tops and base of 9 in., tip 504 on base of 12 in. cake.

Place flowers on cake tops and trim with tip 352 leaves.

Push Swirls into cake top. *Serves 72.*

Heaven Sent

Charming cherubs are linked with a fabulous flower chain. For a monochromatic effect, plates and pillars are "painted" to match.

- 6, 8, 14 in. Round Pans
- Decorating Tips 3, 16, 17, 18, 32, 224
- 10 in. Round Plates
- Dancing Cherub Pillars
- Cake Dividing Set
- Cake Circles
- Fanci-Foil Wrap
- Dowel Rods
- Icing Colors: Orange mixed with Pink
- Wedding Ornament: *Romance & Ruffles*
- Nylon thread (2 ft.)

With thinned royal icing, "paint" pillars and separator plates. Let dry. Make 200 tip 224 drop flowers with tip 3 dot centers. Let dry. With dots of royal icing, secure nylon thread between two flowers, spacing them ½ in. apart on the 2 ft. thread.

Prepare 2-layer cakes for stacked and pillar construction. Using Cake Dividing Set, mark sides of 6 and 8 in. cakes into 8ths, 12 in. into 12ths.

Edge 6 in. base with tip 16 shells; remaining bases with tip 18 rosette borders. Pipe tip 18 fleur-de-lis on 6 in. sides. Add tip 32 columns to 8 and 12 in. sides. Connect fleur-de-lis and columns with tip 17 zigzag garlands. Overpipe with tip 3 triple drop strings. Trim points of garlands with tip 17 rosettes and add flowers.

Edge cake tops with tip 32 shell borders. Trim edge of separator plate with tip 17 e-motion.

At reception, position tiers on pillars. Attach garland of flowers to cherub's hands with dots of glue. Add Romance & Ruffles.
Serves 102.

Inspiration

This stunning tribute to love does require patience, but when it's done it will be totally unforgettable! The dimensional effect is achieved by overpiping designs several times with different sizes of decorating tips. Traditionally, the English overpiped cake was made out of fruit cake, then covered with marzipan, iced and decorated with royal icing. Our Snow-White Buttercream Icing will give you satisfactory results for both frosting and decorating. If a pound cake is used, the storage time is approximately 1 week.

- 6, 10, 14 in. Round Pans
- Decorating Tips 1, 2, 3, 4, 14, 16, 101s, 101, 352
- Flower Nail No. 9
- Cake Dividing Set
- Floating Tier Cake Stand
- Cake Circles
- Scroll Pattern (see pattern index)
- Icing Color: Burgundy
- Cake Ornament: *Bisque Porcelain Couple*

Note: To avoid decorations from shifting or collapsing from the weight of the moist icing, pipe no more than one row at a time and allow work to dry completely. On larger cakes icing will usually be dry by the time you've gone around the cake.

Using tip 4 to pipe base, make 30 tip 101s and 50 tip 101 two-tone roses.

Ice 2-layer cakes on cake circles cut to fit. Note: Design is repeated on all tiers (except top of 6 in.), only the number of divisions and sizes of tips will vary. Overpiping should be done on the outer edge of the previous line.

Top of 6 in. tier: Using Cake Dividing Set, divide into 6ths. Mark scroll pattern. Outline scrolls with tip 14 tight zigzags. Overpipe with tip 14 straight line. Then overpipe four more times with tips 4, 3, 2 and 1.

Mark the following divisions on cake tops: 10 in. into 10ths, 1 in. from the edge; 14 in. cake into 12ths, 1¼ in. from edge. With toothpick, draw scallops from mark to mark. Working towards center, mark six more rows of scallops, each ¼ in. apart. Starting from the inner row, cover scallops using the following sequences of tips:
Row A Tip 1.
Row B Tips 2, 1.
Row C Tips 3, 2, 1.
Row D Tips 4, 3, 2, 1.
Row E Tips 16, 4, 3, 2, 1.
Row F Tips 16 zigzags overpiped with tips 16, 4, 3, 2, 1.
Pipe tip 1 dots at all points. Trim center of designs with tip 1 burgundy u-motion.

For garland at top of sides, mark the following divisions 1½ in. from top–6 in. cake into 6ths, 10 in. cake into 10ths and 14 in. cake into 12ths. Pipe tip 2 drop strings from mark to mark. Cover guidelines with tip 16 zigzag garlands. Fill in area above garlands with tip 16 zigzags. Frame zigzag garlands with overpiped drop strings–at top use tips 3, 3, 2, 2, 1, 1; bottom use tips 2, 2, 1, 1. Under garlands pipe tip 1 drop string and burgundy u-motion scallops. Trim points with tip 1 dots.

At bases: Edge the base of each tier with tip 16 zigzags. Following same divisions, mark a garland 1¼ in. above base, then add two more marks ¼ in. apart above first marks in this order. For the bottom row, drop a string with tip 4, then overpipe with tips 4, 3, 3, 2, 2, 1. Middle row: tips 3, 3, 2, 2, 1. Top row: tips 2, 2. Add tip 1 burgundy u-motion scallops. Trim points of garlands with tip 1 dots.

Edge the base of each tier with tip 16 zigzags. Attach flowers (allow space on top tier for couple) with dots of icing. Trim with tip 352 white leaves. Place cakes on cake stand and position couple*. *Serves 95.*

*At reception.

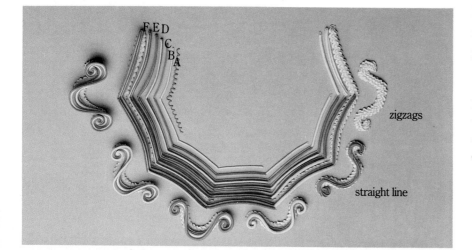
zigzags
straight line

Beaded Lace

Graceful scallops inset with dainty lace—easy to do yet so impressive to view. Beaded leaves add an elegant touch.

- 6, 10, 14 in. Round Pans
- Decorating Tips 4, 2, 7, 12, 67, 103, 104
- Flower Nail No. 7
- 16 in. Round Separator Plates
- 12 in. Lacy-Look Pillars
- Kolor-Flo Fountain
- Floral Accents, Pearl Leaves
- Cake Dividing Set
- Dowel Rods
- Cake Circles
- Wedding Ornament: *Lustrous Love*

Make 8 tips 12 and 104 roses; 6 each tips 12 and 103 roses, tip 103 sweet peas and tip 104 half roses; 12 tip 103 rosebuds.

Prepare 2-layer cakes for stacked construction. Using cake dividing set, with toothpick, dot mark 6 in. tier into 3rds. Divide each section into 3rds again. Mark 10 in. cake into 12ths. Mark 14 in. sides into 4ths. Divide each 4th into 4ths. Mark garlands on sides, angling them on sides of top and bottom tier.

Cover lower portion of sides with tip 2 cornelli lace. Pipe tip 104 garland drape on sides.

Edge tops with tip 4 and bases with tip 7 bead borders.

Push beaded leaves into cake sides. Attach roses and flower cascades on sides with dots of icing. Pipe tip 67 leaves.

At reception: Attach Floral Puffs to pillars. Position fountain and place cake on pillars. Arrange flowers around fountain. Position Lustrous Love. *Serves 116.*

Sonata

This trio makes beautiful music together. A stairway of satiny rolled fondant, intriquing lacy-look "sotas" (a cornelli-like Philippine technique done by piping touching curls, V's and C's of icing randomly) and lush orchids are the epitomy of elegance.

- 4 Pc. Oval Pan Set (use 3 largest pans)
- Decorating Tips 1, 5
- Dowel Rods
- Cake Circles, Tuk 'N Ruffle, Fanci-Foil Wrap
- Stairway Pattern (see pattern index)
- Crystal-Look Bowl
- Bisque Bridal Couple
- Fresh flowers (have florist arrange top bouquet in Crystal-Look Bowl)

Prepare 2-layer cakes for stacked construction. Stack cakes together with backs aligned.

To cover stairs, you'll need a ½ recipe of Rolled Fondant. Using Stairway Pattern, cut stairs out of rolled fondant.

Cover sides and tops of cakes with tip 1 sotas (add 1 tsp. of light corn syrup to each cup of buttercream icing for better piping consistency). Edge stairway and cake bases with tip 5 bead borders.

Arrange flowers around base. Position bouquet on top and push orchid into cake side. Add bisque couple.
Serves 114.

Crowning Touch

Sinuous stringwork, graceful garlands, precise shell borders are dotted with one-squeeze rosette posies. Isn't it amazing such an easy, quick technique can look so stunning?

- 6, 10, 14 in. Round Pans
- Decorating Tips 4, 13, 16, 17, 32, 349, 364,
- Crystal-Clear Cake Divider Set Plates (8 & 12 in.) & 7½ in. Twist Legs
- Cake Dividing Set
- Cake Circles, Fanci-Foil Wrap
- Icing Colors: Pink, Leaf Green
- Wedding Ornament: *Hearts A Flutter*

Prepare 2-layer cakes for push-in pillar construction. Mark position of legs on cake top.

Using Cake Dividing Set, with toothpick, mark 6 & 10 in. cake sides into 8ths, 14 in. into 12ths. Using these marks as a guide, mark scallop design on cake tops— approximately 2½ in. from edge of 10 in. cake, 3 in. from 14 in. edge.

Pipe zigzag garlands on sides–tip 16 on 6 in. tip 17 on 10 & 14 in.

Edge cake bases with tip 32 shell borders. Add tip 32 upright shells (approximately 1½ in. long) to 10 in. base (add as shell border is piped).

Pipe tip 4 drop strings on 10 and 14 in. tops and sides. Edge 6 and 14 in. cake tops with tip 32 upright shell crown border. Pipe tip 364 shell border on 10 in. cake top.

Trim garlands, shells and cake tops with tip 16 rosettes. Finish ends of garland on 10 in. tier with tip 13 shells. Add tip 349 leaves. Position Hearts A Flutter.
Serves 116.

Rose Majesty

*Cascades of dainty mini roses add enormous
impact to this classic, ruffled masterpiece.*

- 6 & 10 in. Round Pans
- 14 in. Square Pans
- Decorating Tips 4, 6, 101, 102, 103, 124, 352, 362, 364
- Flower Nail No. 9
- 12 in. Round Separator Plates
- 7 in. Corinthian Pillars
- Heart Bowl Vase
- Cake Dividing Set
- Cake Circles & Boards
- Fanci Foil Wrap
- Dowel Rods
- Icing Colors: Orange or Creamy Peach, Moss Green
- Wedding Ornament: *Satin Elegance*

You'll need 180 mini roses—make 90 each tips 6 and 101 and tips 6 and 102.

Prepare 2-layer cakes for stacked and pillar construction. Using Cake Dividing Set, divide round cakes into 8ths. Divide each side of square into 3rds. Connect marks on 6 in. sides with tip 4 double drop strings.

Pipe tip 364 e-motion border around separator plate. Add tip 124 ruffle garlands on sides of 10 in. round and square. Edge 10 in. base with tip 124 ruffle (pipe flat on plate). Trim ruffle with tip 124 shells.

Trim garlands with tip 362 swirled shells. Add tip 4 double drop strings to garlands. Edge cake tops with tip 362 swirled shells, bases with tip 364 shells. Trim swirled shells on 6 in. cake top with tip 102 fluted flounce.

Fill vase with icing. Add roses. Trim tiers with roses. Add tip 352 leaves. Position Satin Elegance. *Serves 137.*

3-Tier Wedding Cheesecake

3-Tier Cheesecake Recipe

Cheesecake is becoming a very popular choice. This luscious recipe is from The Cake Bible by Rose Beranbaum*.

10 (8-ounce) packages cream cheese
5 cups sugar
⅓ cup cornstarch
15 large eggs
(3 cups)
¾ cup lemon juice, freshly squeezed
2½ Tbsps. vanilla
1¼ tsp. salt
15 cups (3 qts. plus 3 cups) sour cream

Use 12 in., 10 in. and 6 in. cake pans, each 3 in. deep, plus 3 large pans to serve as water baths. (The sides of the water bath pans must be 3 in. or under or baking will be slowed.) Grease the baking pans and line the bottoms with parchment or waxed paper.

To Mix Batter

Arrange oven racks as close to the center of the oven as possible with at least 4 in. between them. Preheat oven to 350°.

In a mixing bowl, beat cream cheese and sugar, preferably with flat beater, until very smooth (about 3 minutes). Beat in the cornstarch. Beat in the eggs, 1 at a time, scraping down sides of the bowl until smooth. Add the lemon juice, vanilla and salt and beat until mixed. Beat in sour cream just until blended.

Pour the filling into the prepared pans. Set the pans into the larger pans. Fill larger pans with at least 1 in. hot water. Bake in preheated oven for 50 minutes. Turn off the oven and allow the cakes to cool in oven without opening the door for 1 hour. Remove to racks and cool to room temperature (1 hour for the smaller layers, longer for the larger one). Cover with plastic wrap and refrigerate overnight.

Recipe requires a 5-quart mixer large enough to handle the batter in 2 batches. It can also be prepared in several batches in a food processor.

Note: Use glass measuring cups.

To Unmold:

Have ready, matching size cake circles. Attach to Floating Tier Stand Plates with icing.

Run a thin-blade metal spatula between pan and cake, making sure to press well against the sides of the pan. Place pan on heated burner for 10 to 20 seconds, moving it back and forth. Place prepared plate against pan and invert. Remove pan and parchment. If cake does not release, return to the hot burner for a few more seconds.

Refrigerate until ready to frost with White Cream Cheese Icing (recipe follows).

Store:

Three days refrigerated before frosting or decorating; 24 hour refrigerated after decorating. Texture is changed by freezing.

Serve:

Lightly chilled.

*Used with permission of William Morrow & Co.

White Cream Cheese Icing

Ideal for frosting tiers and piping simple decorations.

24 ounces White Candy Melts
4 (8-ounce) packages cream cheese, softened
2 cups unsalted butter, softened
¼ cup lemon juice, freshly squeezed

Melt Candy Melts according to package directions. Allow the coating to cool slightly, stirring occasionally (don't let it set up).

In a mixing bowl, beat the cream cheese (preferably with a flat beater) until smooth and creamy. Gradually beat in the cooled coating until smoothly blended. Beat in the butter and lemon juice.

Store:

1 day room temperature, 2 weeks refrigerated 2 months frozen. Allow to come to room temperature before rebeating otherwise icing may curdle.

Hints:

Buttercream may separate slightly if room temperature is very warm. This can be corrected by setting the bowl in ice water and whisking mixture. The buttercream becomes spongy on standing. Rebeat to restore smooth creamy texture.

Use ice to chill your hands during piping to maintain firm texture.

To Decorate:

• Decorating Tip 21
• Floating Tier Cake Stand
• Cake Circles
• 7 pints of medium size strawberries (extras may be served alongside), cleaned and dry, a jar of strawberry glaze, pastry brush

Ice cakes smooth with White Chocolate Buttercream Icing. Coat cake tops with a thin layer of strawberry glaze. Cover tops with half and whole (in center) strawberries. Brush with strawberry glaze.

Edge tops with tip 21 "fleur-v-lis" (no center shell). Edge bases with tip 21 comma-motion shells.
Serves 150. Note: Portions are smaller than regular wedding cake servings. Top tier is served, not saved.

Courtly Cotillion shown
(instructions follow)

Wedding Cakes

Over 150 Servings

Courtly Cotillion

Shown on preceding page.

Intricate drop strings gracefully go around. Fancy fleur-de-lis stand out like jewels in a royal crown. The lovely tiers are linked together with cascading ribbon streamers.

- 6 x 3 in. Round Pan
- 10, 16 in. Round Pans
- Decorating Tips 3, 12, 17, 18, 21, 104, 107, 352
- Flower Nail No. 7
- 12 in. Round Separator Plates
- Expandable Pillars
- Cake Circles, Tuk 'N Ruffle, Fanci-Foil Wrap
- Dowel Rods
- Icing Color: Royal Blue
- Wedding Ornament: *Look of Love* 8 yds. ribbon (cut into 3 ft. pieces)

Make 35 tips 12 and 104 roses; 45 tip 107 drop flowers with tip 3 dot centers.

Ice and prepare one-layer 6 in., 2-layer 10 in. and 16 in. cakes for stacked and pillar construction. Ice four 2-layer cakes on Tuk 'n Ruffle-trimmed, foil-covered cake circles.

Mark cakes at the following intervals: 6 in. 2½ ins.; 10 in., 3 ins.; 16 in. at 3½ in. (marks should be centered on side of 16 in. cake).

Connect marks with tip 3 overlapping drop strings (single, double and triple strand combinations).

Pipe tip 18 fleur-de-lis around base of 10 in. tier, tops of 10 in. satellite cakes and side of 16 in. Trim 16 in. fleur-de-lis

with tip 3 dots. Edge tops and bases with shell border adding an upright "comma-motion" shell at bases of 6 and 10 in. cakes. Use tip 17 on 6 in., tip 18 for top borders and tip 21 at bases of remaining cakes.

Edge separator plate with tip 18 e-motion border. Attach flowers to cake tops. Also attach ribbon streamers to top tier. Trim flowers with tip 352 leaves.

At reception, position Look of Love on plate. Add expandable pillars (10 in. high) and stacked tiers. Arrange satellite cakes and attach ribbons with dots of icing. *Serves 295.*

Florentine Flair

Bold scrolls and bands, overpiped with stunning contrast, have commanding impact on these tiers of tradition.

- Oval Pan Set (2 smaller size pans are used)
- 11 x 15, 12 x 18 in. Sheet Pans
- Decorating Tips 1D, 3, 15, 21, 102
- 8½ in. Oval Separator Plates
- 5 in. Grecian Pillars
- Rosy Puff Accents (2 needed)
- Cake Boards, Tuk 'N Ruffle, Fanci-Foil Wrap
- Dowel Rods
- Icing Color: Leaf Green
- Wedding Ornament: *Devotion*

Ice and prepare 2-layer cakes for stacked and pillar construction.

Pipe tip 15 swirled shells around separator plate. Edge tops of ovals and base tier with tip 1D ribbed stripe bands. With toothpick, mark ¾ in. intervals on bands. At marks, overpipe bands with tip 15. Use a zigzag motion when piping the contrasting "s-stripe."

Pipe tip 3 drop strings on sides of base tier. Trim points of strings with tip 3 beads.

Mark 1½ in. up from all bases and down from top of sheets. Pipe tip 21 "comma-motion" scrolls (invert for top border). Space approximately ½ in. apart. Overpipe tails of scrolls on top tier and 11 x 15 in. with tip 15 zigzags. Trim zigzags with tip 102 ruffles. Dot center of all scrolls with tip 15 stars.

Position top tier on pillars. Add floral puffs and Devotion. *Serves 220.*

Westminster

*The gothic grandeur is breathtaking to behold.
Our Wedding Cake Cathedral Kit is combined
with round and square tiers for a meaningful,
monumental tribute to the sanctity of marriage.*

- 6, 8, 16 in. Square Pans
- 12 in. Round Pans
- Decorating Tips 2, 2A, 4, 8, 10, 347
- Wedding Cake Cathedral Kit
- 7 in. Square Separator Plates
- Cake Boards, Fanci-Foil Wrap
- Dowel Rods
- Petite Classic Couple
- Porcelain Groomsmen & Bridesmaids*
  (4 of each)
- Gothic Patterns (see pattern index)
- 6 in. square or round piece of wood
  (cover with white foil or styrofoam to
  support center tiers, electric night light
  socket, 15 watt bulb, extension cord, ¼
  in. thick piece of fiberboard to support
  16 in. square, silk flower bouquets
  (4 needed)

*Paint gowns desired color.

Assemble cathedral components according to directions included with your kit. Using royal icing, edge steeple, archway and chapel with tip 347 outlines. Note: As you pipe with tip 347, hold the tip with single hole up and the double holes down for effect shown. Trim lines with tip 2 dots.

Ice 2-layer cakes (one of each size square and five 12 in. rounds) on boards and circles cut to fit. Prepare 8 in. square, 12 in. round and 16 in. square for stacked construction.

With toothpick, mark Gothic Arch Patterns on all cake sides. On 6 in. & 12 in. satellite cakes, outline arches (patterns A1 & A2) with tip 347. Outside of outline, pipe tip 4 outline. Pipe tip 2 dots inside of arch.

For corner design on 6 in. sides, outline marks with tip 4. Overpipe 2 more times. Pipe tip 4 outline inside.

On 8 & 16 in. squares, cover arches with tip 347. Above outline, pipe another outline with tip 4. Trim points of arches with tip 4 dots.

On 12 in. round, outline both arch designs with tip 349. Pipe lines around designs and scrolls inside triple arch with tip 4. Trim arches with tip 2 dots.

Trim corners of square cakes with tip 2A upright shells. With tip 4, overpipe shells with 5 lines. Add tip 2 dots to shells and down sides.

Edge cake tops with tip 8 triple bead borders. Pipe tip 10 bulb borders on all bases.

Assemble cakes (at reception) according to instructions included with the cathedral kit. Position couple and wedding party. Add nosegays to cake tops.
Serves 440.

Golden Venice

Our stunning spectacular was inspired by the "Bridge of Sighs" in Italy. Flower-strewn stairways lift the happy couple to breathtaking heights. Tiny lights and glowing fountain illuminate this ultra-romantic tiered trio.

- 8 & 14 in. Round Pans
- Decorating Tips 3, 5, 7, 11, 101, 102, 103, 352
- 10 in. Round Separator Plates (2 sets needed)
- 9 in. Round Separator Plate
- 7 in. Corinthian Pillars
- Filigree Platform & Stairway Set
- Filigree Fountain Frame
- Kolor-Flo Fountain
- Fountain Cascade Set
- Garden Gazebo
- 4½ in. Bisque Porcelain Couple
- Frolicking Cherubs (2 needed)
- Cake Dividing Set
- Cake Circles, Fanci-Foil Wrap
- 15 Pc. Decorator Pattern Press Set
- Nylon thread, battery-operated miniature lights

Using royal icing, make 150 tip 101, 250 tip 102 and 500 tip 103 sweet peas. To pipe flowery vines: Secure waxed paper to the back of a cookie sheet or cake board with dots of icing. To it, tape 13 strands of 20 in. long nylon thread (fold in half) tautly. Pipe tip 101 and some 102 sweet peas (spacing ¼ to ½ in. apart) directly on thread. Let dry completely. Cut one strand in half for cherubs to hold.

Ice and prepare 2-layer cakes for pillar construction. Also dowel rod 14 in. center cake to support fountain, then postion 9 in. separator plate.

Using Cake Dividing Set, divide center 14 in. cake into 12ths, remaining tiers into 8ths. With scroll pattern press, imprint scrolls on two 14 in. cakes. Cover marks with tip 5.

Pipe double bead garlands with tip 3. Trim garlands on 8 in. cakes with tip 3 dots; garlands on 14 in. center tier with tip 3 bows.

Edge separator plates with tip 11 e-motion borders. Edge tiers with bead borders–tops of 8 in. with tip 7, bases of 8 in. and tops of 14 in. cakes with tip 11. Pipe tip 7 triple bead borders at bases of 14 in. cakes.

Attach Frolicking Cherubs to plates with royal icing. Position Stairway and Platform together. Place Garden Gazebo on platform. Tape battery for lights onto platform. Wind lights and flowers vines onto stairways. Attach a short strand of vines to cherubs, flowers to platform, gazebo and cherubs with dots of royal icing. Place flowers on cakes. Trim with tip 352 leaves.

At reception, arrange cakes together. Place fountain, cascade and frame on center cake. Position tiers on pillars. Add stairways. Position couple. *Serves 256.*

Ruffles and Lace

These pretty petals and classic rounds are bound to astound. Richly adorned with dainty and bold icing decor and delicate glass ornament.

- 6, 12 in. Petal Pans
- 8, 16 in. Round Pans
- Decorating Tips 2, 3, 16, 17, 18, 19, 103, 104, 125, 224, 352
- 7 & 9 in. Crystal-Look Plates
- 7 & 9 in. Crystal-Look Spiked Pillars
- Rosy Puff Accents (2 needed)
- Cake Dividing Set
- Cake Circles, Fanci-Foil Wrap
- Dowel Rods
- Heart & Curved Triangle Patterns (see pattern index)
- Icing Color: Violet
- Wedding Ornament: *Hearts A Flutter*

Make 50 tip 224 drop flowers with tip 3 dot centers.

Prepare and ice 2-layer cakes for stacked and spiked pillar construction. Using Cake Dividing Set, with toothpick, dot mark sides of round cakes–8 in. into 8ths, 16 in. into 20ths. Mark Heart Pattern and flower stems on sides of 8 in. cake, Curved Triangle Pattern on sides of petals. Also mark scallops (1½ in. deep) on top of 16 in. cake and a 7½ in. diameter circle on top of 12 in.

Cover hearts, triangles, 12 and 16 in. (background areas) cake tops with tip 2 cornelli lace. On petals, pipe pairs of upright shells– tip 17 on 6 in., tip 19 on 12 in. Edge hearts with tip 103 and triangles on 12 in. petal with tip 104 ruffles. Outline triangles and hearts with tip 17.

Edge petal tops and bases with tip 17 zig-zag puff borders. Outline scallops on 16 in. cake top with tip 16. Trim puffs and shells with tip 17 rosettes.

Pipe tip 3 outline stems and tip 352 leaves on sides on 8 in. cake. Edge 16 in. base with tip 125 double ruffle border. Pipe tip 18 e-motion shell border at bases of round cakes.

Edge circle on 12 in. top and base of 8 in. round with tip 17 shell border. Pipe tip 18 "comma-motion" shell borders around tops of 8 and 16 in. cakes. Trim shells on 16 in. with tip 104 ruffles. Add flowers to sides and trim with tip 352 leaves.

Push pillars into cakes at reception and position cakes. Add Rosy Puff Accents and Hearts A Flutter.
Serves 162.

Floral Sparklers

Brilliant bursts of Philippine-Method blooms are dancing on air. Pretty ruffles in contrasting hues add romance.

- 8, 16 in. Square Pans
- 12 in. Round Pans
- Decorating Tips 5, 16, 19, 45, 55, 59, 103, 124
- 10 & 14 in. Round Separator Plates (2 of each size needed)
- Expandable Pillars
- Cake Circles & Boards
- Fanci-Foil Wrap
- Tuk 'N Ruffle
- Heart Bowl Vase
- Dowel Rods
- Florist Wire
- Icing Color: Pink
- Wedding Ornament: *Ecstasy*
- White floral tape, ribbon

With royal icing, pipe the following flowers on wires. 30 each white, light and dark pink tips 5 and 103 roses; 30 each tips 5 and 45 rosebuds in same shades as roses. 100 white dama de noche done with tips 5 and 55. Tip 59 sampaquita sprays in pink and white, 25 of each. You will need to make 5 bouquets, fill vase and accent Ecstasy with these flowers.

Ice and prepare 2-layer cakes for pillar construction (8 in. square is placed on 10 in. round separator plates). Using Cake Dividing Set, with toothpick, mark 12 in. cake into 10ths. Divide sides of 8 in. in half; 16 in. into 4ths.

Edge base of 16 in. cake with tip 19 shell border. Pipe tip 124 ruffle garlands on sides—two rows on 8 and 10 in. tiers; three rows on 16 in.

Pipe tip 16 e-motion around separator plate. Edge cake tops with tip 16 shell borders.

Edge 8 and 12 in. bases with tip 19 e-motion borders. At 8 in. cake base, add tip 124 ruffle next to border on plate. Trim e-motion base borders and sides of 16 in. cake (at garland points) with tip 16 stars.

When assembling tiers, position Ecstasy before adding pillars (10 in. high). Add 12 in. tier, vase and pillars (9 in. high). Set 8 in. cake atop pillars and add bouquet. Push flowers into 16 in. cake.
Serves 184.

Daisy Belle

Count on these daisies to tell that two are in love.
Sunny yellow and white "petals with pull" and
delicate ferns peek out of openwork bells. Icing dots
on tops and sides resemble "dotted swiss."

- 6, 8, 10, 14 x 3 in. Round Pans
- Decorating Tips 3, 4, 16, 103, 349
- Flower Nail No. 7
- Tall Tier Cake Stand (8, 10, 12 and 18 in. plates are used)
- Cake Corer
- 2 in. Filigree Bells (4 packages)
- Cake Circles
- Flower Formers
- Edible Glitter
- Florist Wire
- Cake Dividing Set
- Icing Colors: Lemon Yellow, Moss Green
- Wedding Ornament: *Wedding Bells*
- Fresh flowers

You'll need 50 daisies—25 of each color (white and yellow) tip 103 daisies with tip 4 dot centers. Pat centers with edible glitter. Let dry on flower formers. Optional: make 25 more daisies to accent greenery at base.

Using tips 3 and 349, make 80 ferns on florist wires. Push into styrofoam block to dry.

Cut a center hole in cake circles (use cake corer as a guide). Ice cakes smooth on circles. Core out centers of 8, 10 and 14 in. cakes with cake corer. Attach 7¾ in. columns in 10, 12 and 18 in. plates. Place cakes (except 6 in.) on separator plates. Note: 6 in. cake can be placed on cake circle slightly larger so decorating can be done.

Using Cake Dividing Set, with toothpick, mark cakes from top tier to bottom tier into the following divisions—6ths, 8ths, 10ths and 12ths.

Draw scalloped guidelines from mark to mark. Outline scallops on top and pipe drop strings on sides with tip 16.

Trim inside of garlands on 6 and 10 in. tiers and cover tops and sides of 8 in. and 14 in. cakes with tip 3 dots.

Edge cake tops with tip 16 reverse shell borders. Pipe tip 16 e-motion border at bases (except 6 in.; it will be decorated after assembly).

Attach flowers and ferns to sides. As you assemble tiers, position bells, flowers and ferns on each cake as you work up*.

Anchor 8 in. plate with column cap nut and position 6 in. cake. Edge base with tip 16 e-motion border. Arrange greenery and attach icing daisies around base. Position Wedding Bells. *Serves 84*

Note: To increase servings, use 2-layer cakes or torte and fill 3 in. tiers. This will increase servings to 172.

*To serve, start cutting with the top tier.

Reflections

Here's an ingenious way to serve many with a minimal amount of work. This fascinating double-take mates a couple of Floating Tier Cake Stands together in perfect harmony. Ribbon bows and bands tie the knot beautifully.

- 6, 8, 10, 14 in. Round Pans
- Decorating Tips 8, 12
- Floating Tiers Cake Stand (two needed)
- Pearl Leaf Puffs (8 needed)
- 2 in. Iridescent Bells (12 used)
- Florist Wire (for making bows)
- Cake Circles, Tuk 'N Ruffle, Fanci-Foil Wrap
- Wedding Ornament: *Lustrous Love*
- Iridescent ribbon (20 ft. of ½ in. & 34 ft. of 1¼ in. wide ribbon) Pedestal cake stand to hold 8 in. cake between tiered cakes.

Make 7 bows with narrow ribbon. To make: Make a small center loop. Twist at base of loop and then form side loop. Twist at base of loop and make loop on other side. Repeat procedure three more times. Join loops by twisting a piece of florist wire in center. Allow enough wire to push bow into cake.

Cut two each 1, 6 and 8 ft. bands and one 2 ft. band from wider ribbon.

With florist wire, attach two bells to each Pearl Leaf Puff.

Ice 2-layer cakes (one 8 in. and two each 6, 10 and 14 in.) on cake circles and Tuk 'N Ruffle trimmed plates.

Edge cake bases with tip 12 e-motion borders; tops with tip 8 fleur-de-lis borders.

Attach ribbon bands with dots of icing. Push bows into cake.

At reception, assemble plates on Floating Tier Stand. Position 8 in. cake on pedestal cake stand. Place belled puffs and Lustrous Love on cake tops.
Serves 194.

Lady Windemere III

An illustrious trio and glorious quartet compose this classical medley. Curvacious scrolls, bold borders and jaunty wild roses join together in perfect harmony.

- 6, 10, 14 in. Round Pans
- Decorating Tips 2, 4, 14, 16, 18, 102, 104
- Flower Nail No. 7
- Tall Tier Stand Set plus these additional pieces–7¾ in. column, 4 more 12 in. plates
- Tall Tier 4-Arm Base Stand
- Cake Corer
- Cake Circles
- Cake Dividing Set
- 15 pc. Pattern Press Set
- 2 in. Satin Bells (3 packages)
- Scroll Patterns (see pattern index)
- Icing Color: Golden Yellow, Brown (mix together for ivory), Creamy Peach
- Wedding Ornament: *Look of Love*

Make 50 tip 104 and 24 tip 102 wild roses with tip 2 pull-out dots in the centers.

Cut center holes in one 6 in. , 10 in. and a 14 in. cake circle. Ice 2-layer cakes (five 10 in. rounds are needed) smooth. Core out centers of one of the 10 in. and 14 in. cakes. Position column sections.

Using Cake Dividing Set, mark 6 in. cake into 4ths, 10 in. cakes into 8ths and 14 in. cake into 16ths. Imprint sides of 6 in. and 14 in. cakes with 2 in. C-scroll pattern press. Mark Scroll Patterns on 10 in. and 14 in. cake tops.

Pipe tip 16 C-scrolls. Between cake top scrolls, add tip 18 elongated shells. Trim tails with tip 16 rosettes. Add tip 16 side shells to scrolls on 6 in. and 14 in. sides.

For garlands on 10 in. cakes, drop a tip 4 guideline from mark to mark (1½ in. deep). Pipe tip 18 zigzag garlands. Fill in area above garlands with tip 18 zigzags. Overpipe with tip 4 triple drop strings. On 6 in. and 14 in. sides, pipe tip 4 double drop string garlands (approximately 1½ in. wide).

Edge cake tops and around cored centers with tip 16 shell borders. On all cakes except 6 in., pipe tip 18 zigzag puffs (approximately 1½ in. wide) at bases. Above puffs, add tip 14 zigzags. Position bells on four 10 in. cakes. Attach flowers to bells and cakes with dots of icing.

At reception, place base bolt through 4-Arm Stand center and anchor bolt to 7¾ in. column. Position 10 in. cakes on 4-Arm Base Stand. Assemble center tiers. Anchor in. plate with column cap nut. Position 6 in. cake and edge base same as other tiers were done. Position Look of Love.
Serves 273.

Hearts

Shimmery stairways take you down the most romantic aisle of wedding tiers around.

- 6, 8, 10, 14 in. Round Pans
- Decorating Tips 18, 88
- 9 & 11 in. Crystal Look Plates
  (1 set of each size)
- Crystal-Look Tier Set
- 3 & 7 in. Crystal-Look Pillars
  (4 of each size)
- Crystal-Look Bowls (4 needed)
- Crystal Stairways (3 needed)
- 5½ in. Crystal-Look Hearts (4 used)
- 9-pc. Pattern Press Set
- Cake Circles
- Cake Dividing Set
- Dowel Rods
- Bisque Couple
- 2 yds. 1½ in. wide satin ribbon, fresh
  flowers

When you order floral arrangements, bring Crystal-Look Bowls, Hearts and Bisque Couple. The two parts of the bowl are used as individual vases. Glue ribbon to stairs.

Prepare two 6 in.; one 8 in.; two 10 in.; one 14 in. 2-layer cakes for stacked construction. Using Cake Dividing Set, mark 6 in. cakes into 4ths and all the rest into 8ths.

Imprint sides of 6 and 14 in. cakes with scroll heart pattern press. Cover marks with tip 18 scrolls. Pipe tip 18 fleur-de-lis on sides of 10 in. cakes. Trim sides at bases with tip 18 swirled shell "v's."

Pipe tip 88 ruffle garlands on sides. Edge cake tops with tip 18 shell borders. Edge bases with tip 88 ruffle borders (double ruffle at base of 14 in. cake).

At reception, position cakes on pillars with flowers. Arrange cakes and add stairways. Place bouquets on cake tops and at foot of stairway.
Serves 194.

Duchess

*The perfect blending for a storybook wedding
Adoring hearts surround regal tiers. Lovely
bouquets and intricate strings lavishly adorn.*

- 6 & 9 in. Heart Pans
- 6 & 14 in. Round Pans
- Decoratings Tips 1, 3, 14, 16, 17, 47, 103, 131, 199
- Flower Nail No 7 and Lily Nail
- 7 in. Heart Separator Plates
- 16 in. Round Separator Plates
- 13 in. Arched Pillars
- 7 in. Corinthian Pillars
- Yellow Stamens
- Florist Wire
- Dowel Rods
- Cake Boards, Circles, Fanci-Foil Wrap
- Wedding Ornament: *Reflection*
- ½ in wide ribbon, styrofoam for large bouquet bases, white florist tape

For two large bouquets on heart tiers, you'll need to pipe on florist wire 15 each petunias and leaves, 13 wild roses and 25 drop flowers. Push into styrofoam bases. For two small bouquets on 14 in. round, pipe on wires, 4 petunias, 5 wild roses, 6 drop flowers and 6 leaves. Place ribbon bow on wires. When flowers dry, twist stems together and cover with florist tape. To decorate ornament, make 6 each petunias and drop flowers, 6 leaves. Twist stems together and attach to ornament with florist tape. To decorate satellite cakes, make 12 petunias, wild roses and 40 drop flowers. Tie ribbon bows.

Make royal icing flowers with the following: Petunias with tip 103 with tip 14 star centers and artificial stamens. Tip 131 drop flowers with tip 3 dot centers. Tip 103 wild rose with tip 1 dot centers. Tip 352 leaves. Pipe flowers and leaves for bouquets and to accent ornament on florist wire.

Ice 2-layer cakes smooth on cake boards and plates as shown. Prepare a 9 in. heart and 14 in. round for stacked construction.

For stringwork, with toothpick, mark the following (approximate) intervals: 2½ in. on 9 in. hearts; 3 in. on 14 in. round; 2 in. on both 6 in. cakes. Pipe tip 3 triple drop strings on 9 in. hearts and overlapping (triple) drop strings on remaining tiers.

Pipe tip 199 double upright shells on 9 in. hearts. Edge 9 in. heart bases and tops of all tiers with tip 17 rosette borders.

Edge remaining bases with tip 199 upright shells. Connect shells on 6 in. heart with tip 3 overlapping drop strings. Trim upright shells at bases with tip 16 rosettes.

Attach flowers and bows to satellite cakes with dots of icing. Trim with tip 352 leaves.

At reception, position Reflection, tiers on pillars, bouquets and satellite cakes. *Serves 211. 6 in. heart or round can be saved.*

Marilyn
James

Lovey-Dovey shown
(instructions follow)

Shower and Anniversary Cakes

Lovey-Dovey

Shown on preceding page.

*Pretty-as-can-be cake 'n candy combination sets
an amorous mood. Bells, roses, hearts and doves
symbolize romantic love.*

- 12 in. Hexagon Pans
- Mini Bell Pan
- Decorating Tips 3, 30, 32, 124
- Pink, Green & White Candy Melts™*
- Wedding Bells, Roses Candy Molds
- Cake Board, Fanci-Foil Wrap, Tuk 'N Ruffle
- Decorator's Brush

Mold 2 bells, a rose, 2 rosebuds and 6 "love dove" hearts out of melted Candy Melts (melting directions are on package).

To make bells: Using a decorator's brush, paint the bottom of bell on the inside of pan (not clapper) with pink coating. Allow to set (about 10 minutes). Fill pan with white coating. After approximately 10 minutes, pour out excess coating. Let set completely.

For roses: Paint centers of roses pink, leaves green. Let set. Fill molds with white and let set per directions. For "love doves:" Fill doves with pink coating. Let set approximately 10 minutes. Pour white coating into hearts and let set hard.

Ice 2-layer cake smooth on foil-covered cake board trimmed with Tuk 'N Ruffle. Pipe tip 32 columns on corners. Edge base with tip 30 rosettes; top with tip 30 shells. Trim corners at top with tip 30 rosettes.

Position bells on cake top. Edge with tip 3 melted coating beads. To decorate with Candy Melts: Let coating set for a few minutes. Fill bag fitted with tip 3.

Pipe tip 124 icing ribbon streamers. Attach candy roses and hearts with dots of icing.
Serves 50.
*brand confectionery coating

Love Blooms

Hopes and dreams all in one basket. Delightful
icing flowers put their pretty heads together to say,
"Have a beautiful wedding day!"

- 12 in. Heart Pans
- Decorating Tips 1, 3, 4, 17, 19, 47, 59°, 101, 104, 352
- Flower Nail No. 7
- Flower Formers
- Edible Glitter
- Cake Board, Fanci-Foil Wrap, Tuk 'N Ruffle
- Script Message Pattern Press
- Icing Colors: Leaf Green, Lemon Yellow, Pink, Creamy Peach, Violet

With royal icing, make 15 tips 4 and 104 daisies; 25 tips 1 and 59° violets; 25 tips 1 and 101 apple blossoms. Pat centers of daisies with edible glitter and allow to dry on flower formers.

Ice 2-layer cake smooth on Tuk 'N Ruffle-trimmed, foil-covered cake board.

Imprint message with script pattern press. Outline with tip 3. Write tip 3 names.

Cover basket area with tip 47 basketweave. Edge top and basket rim with tip 17 rope borders. Pipe tip 19 zigzag puffs at base. Add tip 104 ribbon bow.

Arrange flowers on top and at base. Trim with tip 352 leaves.
Serves 48.

Blissful

*Promise them a rose garden with this
serve-a-crowd sheet cake. Cascading blooms are
fenced in with bold basketweave.*

- 9 x 13 in. Sheet Pans
- Decorating Tips 2B, 3, 6, 12, 21, 67, 104
- Flower Nail No. 7
- Cake Boards, Tuk 'N Ruffle, Fanci-Foil Wrap
- Icing Colors: Pink, Moss Green
- Wedding Ornament: *La Belle Petite*

Pipe 6 tips 12 and 104 roses; 2 tips 6 and 104 small roses; 3 half roses and 12 buds with tip 104.

Ice 2-layer cake smooth. Write names with tip 3. Pipe tip 6 bead heart and add tip 3 scrolls.

Cover sides with tip 2B basketweave. Edge top with tip 21 rope border, base with tip 21 shells.

Arrange flowers on cake top and trim with tip 67 leaves. Position La Belle Petite.
Serves 58.

Opulence

Luscious cocoa buttercream is richly adorned with dark chocolate roses and ruffles. A picture-perfect choice for a tasteful couple.

- Oval Pan Set (largest size pan used for cake)
- Decorating Tips 3, 4, 8, 10, 65, 70, 101, 127
- Oval Cutter Set
- Cake Boards, Fanci-Foil Wrap

Ice 2-layer cake smooth with chocolate buttercream. To darken, add additional squares of unsweetened chocolate and ½ Tbsps. of milk until desired color is reached.

Use 2nd smallest size oval pan to mark oval on cake top. Write tip 3 message. Pipe tip 127 half roses. Add tip 8 sepals, calyxes and outline stems. Add tip 3 outline thorns and leaf stems. Pipe tip 70 leaves.

Using 3½ in. oval cutter, imprint ovals on sides. Dot mark area between ovals in half. Inside ovals (approximately ½ in.) mark rose stems. Pipe tip 101 half roses.

Trim with tip 65 leaves. Outline stems with tip 3.

Connect oval shapes with tip 104 ruffle garlands. Edge garlands and outline ovals with tip 4 beads.

Pipe bead borders – tip 8 around top, tip 10 at base. Add tip 127 ruffle borders. Edge ruffles with tip 4 beads.
Serves 70.

Fantasia

*Their hearts still flutter at the sight of one another.
Our joyful tribute is ideal for lovers.*

- 14 in. Round Pans
- Decorating Tips 1, 3, 4, 5, 6, 16, 32
- 16 in. Round Separator Plates
- 5 in. Grecian Pillars
- Cake Circle
- Flower Stamens
- Flower Formers
- Petal & Butterfly Patterns (see pattern index)
- Icing Colors: Creamy Peach, Lemon Yellow, Violet
- Net or tulle, cotton balls, silk leaves, greenery

To make 6 net flowers and 2 butterflies (very fragile, so make extras), use a thin consistency royal icing and tip 1. Let net pieces dry before assembling.

For flowers: Tape 5 petal patterns to outside curve of a large flower former. Cover pattern with waxed paper and attach net with dots of icing. Fill in flower petals with tip 1 cornelli lace (for strength, "s" and "r" should be touching). Edge petals with tip 1 beads. When dry, overpipe beads on opposite side. To assemble flower, with tip 5 pipe a large ball of green icing in the center of a waxed paper square. Push in petals and cover center with tip 1 dots. Support petals with cotton balls until dry.

For butterfly: On a flat surface, cover patterns with waxed paper and attach net. Outline design with tip 1. Edge with tip 1 beads. When dry, turn over and overpipe. Let dry. To assemble: Pipe a 2 in. long line of stiff consistency royal icing with tip 6 for the body. Immediately insert wings into both sides of body (prop up with cotton balls to dry). Push in artificial stamen (cut to fit) antennas.

Ice 2-layer cake smooth. Pipe message with tip 3. Edge top with tip 32 upright shells. Connect shells with tip 4 overlapping drop strings. Trim with tip 16 stars. Edge base with tip 32 shell border.

To serve, cover separator plate with greenery. Add pillars and position cake. Arrange silk leaves, flowers and butterflies.
Serves 77.

Rosy Romantic

*A lavishment of roses and ruffly sweetheart
garlands make this classic round just perfect for a
perfect couple.*

- 12 in. Round Pans
- Decorating Tips 3, 12, 17, 67, 104, 125
- Flower Nail No. 7
- Cake Dividing Set
- Cake Circle
- Icing Colors: Golden Yellow, Brown
  (add small amounts for ivory shade),
  Creamy Peach, Moss Green

Make roses using light and dark shades
and tips 12 and 104. You'll need 6 (3 of
each shade) full and 8 (2 light peach)
5-petal roses. Using tip 104, make half
roses and 20 rosebuds (equal amounts of
each shade).

Ice 2-layer cake smooth on a cake circle.
Position cake on serving plate.

Using Cake Dividing Set, mark sides (in
center) into 10ths. Connect marks with
tip 104 ruffle garlands. Trim with tip 3
drop strings.

Write tip 3 message on cake top. Edge
with ruffles–tip 104 at top, tip 125 at
base. Trim with tip 17 shell borders.

Pipe tip 3 bead hearts between garlands.
Add tip 3 dots to sides and cake top
border.

Arrange rose spray and trim with tip 67
leaves.
Serves 56.

Wild Rose

The delicate design is reminiscent of a fine china pattern. Perfect for showers and anniversaries.

- 8, 12 in. Round Pans
- Decorating Tips 1, 3, 17, 19, 102, 103, 104, 352
- Flower Nail No 9,
- 10 in. Round Separator Plates
- 3 in. Grecian Pillars
- Cake Circles, Tuk 'N Ruffle, Fanci-Foil Wrap
- Cake Dividing Set
- Dowel Rods
- Rosy Puff Accent (1 needed)
- Icing Colors: Cornflower Blue, Golden Yellow, Moss Green
- Wedding Ornament: *Spring Song*

Make 20 spatula-striped, royal icing wild roses–10 with tip 102 and 10 with tip 103. Add tip 1 pull-out dot centers.

Ice and prepare 2-layer cakes for pillar construction. Using Cake Dividing Set, mark sides into 8ths. Drop tip 3 string guidelines for garlands. Pipe tip 3 scrolls on 12 in. Pipe tip 104 ruffle garlands. Edge with tip 3 e-motion.

Outline scallops on separator plate with tip 17. Edge tops with tip 17 shell borders, bases with tip 19.

Pipe tip 3 vines and stems. Add flowers and trim with tip 352 leaves.

At party, position tier on pillars. Attach flowers to Spring Song with dots of icing. Add Rosy Puff Accent and Spring Song. *Serves 50* without top tier; 80 if top tier is served.

Fond Memories

This elegant fondant-covered heart duet will be a triumph to your decorating talents. Graceful scrolls have a simply stunning effect on the arches of "sotas."

- Puffed Heart Pan
- 12 in. Heart Pans
- Decorating Tips 1s, 2, 9
- Scrolls (16 needed)
- Dowel Rods
- Cake Boards, Fanci-Foil Wrap
- Triangle & Arch Patterns (see pattern index)
- Icing Color: Golden Yellow
- Roses & greenery

Lightly ice puffed heart and 2-layer heart with buttercream icing on cake boards cut to fit. Place 12 in. heart on foil-covered cake board. Cover cakes with rolled fondant. Dowel rod 12 in. tier and position puffed heart.

With a straight pin, mark Triangle Pattern on puffed heart, Arch Pattern on 12 in. sides. Cover area outside of arches on top and sides with tip 1s sotas (add 1 tsp. light corn syrup to each cup of royal icing for piping sotas). Edge arches with tip 2 beads. Outline triangles with tip 2. Trim with tip 2 rows of dots.

Edge bases with tip 9 ball borders. Attach Scrolls to sides with dots of icing. Places roses on cake top.
Serves 60.

Silver Lining

For two who are so together only a gala tribute like this will do. Silver leaves and ribbon bands glisten on this pure white masterpiece. This cake is equally beautiful for a Golden Anniversary celebration. Just substitute gold leaves, gold ribbon and Golden Jubilee.

- 6 & 14 in. Square Pans
- Decorating Tips 3, 8, 12, 21, 32, 102, 104
- Flower Nail No. 7
- 8 in. Square Separator Plates
- 6 in. Arched Pillars
- 1¼ in. Silver Leaves
- Rectangle Cake Boards, Fanci-Foil Wrap, Tuk 'n Ruffle
- Dowel Rods
- Florist Wire
- 3 yards of ribbon, florist tape
- Wedding Ornament: *Silver Jubilee*

On wires, make 50 tips 12 and 104 roses with tip 8 calyxes. Tape silver leaves to wires.

Prepare 2-layer cakes for pillar construction. Place ribbon around tiers.

Edge cake tops with tip 21 shells trimmed with tip 102 ruffles. Pipe tip 32 swirled shells at base. Accent with tip 102 ruffles.

Mound icing on separator plate. Push roses and leaves into icing.

Assemble tier on pillars at party. Position Silver Moments. *Serves 106.*

Beloved

*Red and white vibrantly reflect 40 years of love
and respect. Engaging floral vines, hearts, dots
and roses accentuate this oh so fair tribute.*

- 8 & 12 in. Square Pans
- Decorating Tips 3, 12, 104, 353
- Flower Nail No. 7
- 9 in. Square Separator Plates
- 5 in. Grecian Pillars
- 1⅞ in. White Artificial Leaves (15 needed)
- 15-Pc. Decorator Pattern Press Set
- Heart Cutter Set
- Cake Boards, Fanci-Foil Wrap, Tuk 'N Ruffle
- Dowel Rods
- Icing Color: Watermelon
- Wedding Ornament: *Romance & Ruffles*

Make 15 tips 12 and 104 roses.

Ice 2-layer cakes smooth and prepare them for pillar construction. Using scroll pattern press and two smallest heart cutters, imprint designs on each side. Cover marks with tip 3 outlines. Overpipe hearts with tip 3 e-motion. On ends of scrolls, pipe tip 3 fleur-de-lis (red in centers).

Outline separator plate with tip 353. Edge tops and bases with tip 353 heart border. Trim bases with tip 3 dots.

Mound icing on separator plate and cover with roses. Add artificial leaves.

To serve, position tier on pillars. Add Romance & Ruffles.
Serves 104.

Good As Gold

Their long life together deserves a tribute that's brilliant and grand. Our rose-covered sheet will definitely do for a love that has lasted and seen them through.

- 6 x 3 in. Round Pan
- 11 x 15 in. Sheet Pans
- Decorating Tips 3, 12, 17, 19, 21, 102, 103, 104
- Flower Nail No. 7
- Gold Artificial Leaves (12 large, 36 small)
- Cake Boards, Tuk 'N Ruffle, Fanci-Foil Wrap
- Dowel Rods
- Icing Color: Golden Yellow
- Ornament: *50 Years of Happiness*

You'll need 35 roses–make 5 with tips 12 and 104; 10 with tips 12 and 103; 20 with tips 12 and 102. Also make 16 tip 104 rosebuds and 12 half roses.

Ice 2-layer sheet and 3 in. deep round cakes smooth and prepare them for stacked construction.

Write tip 3 message on side. Edge cake tops with reverse shell borders–tip 17 on 6 in. and tip 19 on sheet. Edge bases with shell borders–tip 17 between cakes and tip 21 at base of sheet.

Position roses on top and at base of sheet. Attach leaves with dots of icing.

At party, place 50 Years of Happiness. *Serves 90.*

Wedding Cake How-To's

Since our cake designs run the gamut from simplified to elaborate, we realize that not just experienced decorators will attempt the baking and the decorating. The maid-of-honor, mother of the bride, even the bride or groom might want to create the cake that symbolizes the "breaking of bread in kinship."

With basic decorating skills, even the novice decorator can achieve impressive results by selecting a simplified design such as Swan Symphony or Reflections.

In this mini decorating course, we've included some of the basics and bravura that will lead you to succeed.

Baking The Perfect Wedding Cake

GREASE   **FLOUR**   **SHAKE**   **PLACE RACK**

These directions are for classic 2-layer cakes.

- Preheat oven to temperature specified in recipe or on packaged mix.

- Thoroughly grease the inside of each pan with solid vegetable shortening or use a vegetable cooking spray. Use a pastry brush to spread the shortening evenly. Be sure sides, corners and all indentations are completely covered.

- Sprinkle flour inside of pan and shake back and forth so the flour covers all the greased surfaces. Tap out excess flour and if any shiny spots remain, touch up with more shortening and flour. This step is essential in preventing your cake from sticking. If you prefer, the bottom may be lined with waxed paper after greasing. This eliminates flouring the pan. Your cake will unmold easily, but with more crumbs.

- Bake the cake according to temperature and time specifications in recipe or on package instructions. Remove cake from oven and let cool 10 minutes in pan on a cake rack. Larger cakes over 12 in. diameter may need to cool 15 minutes.

- So cake sits level and to prevent cracking, while in pan or after unmolding, cut away the raised center portion with serrated knife. Hint: Our Bake-Even Strips help prevent crowns from forming. To unmold cake, place cake rack against cake and turn both rack and pan over. Remove pan carefully. If pan will not release, return it to a warm oven (250°) for a few minutes, then repeat procedure. Cool cake completely, at least 1 hour. Brush off loose crumbs and ice.

Wedding Cake Recipes

White Wedding Cake

6 cups sifted cake flour
2 Tbsps. baking powder
1½ cups butter or margarine
3 cups sugar
2 cups milk
1 tsp. vanilla extract
12 egg whites

Preheat oven to 325°. Grease bottom of pans and line with waxed or parchment paper.

Sift together flour and baking powder. Set aside. Cream butter and sugar together until light and fluffy. Set aside. Beat egg whites until stiff, but not dry. Set aside.

With mixer at slow speed, add flour mixture to butter mixture, alternately with milk. Beat well after each addition. Beat in vanilla extract.

Gently fold egg whites into batter. Pour into prepared pans. Bake until toothpick inserted into center comes out clean.

Yield: 12 cups of cake batter.

One recipe will fill one 14 in. round pan and bakes approximetely 50 minutes at 325°. Check batter chart for other size pans.

Luscious Chocolate Cake
Ideal for grooms' cakes, too.

8 (1-ounce) squares unsweetened
   chocolate
1 cup butter or margarine
2 cups hot water
4 cups sifted cake flour
½ teaspoon salt
2 cups sour cream
2 teaspoons vanilla
1 Tbsp. baking soda
4 eggs, beaten

Grease, flour and line pans with parchment or waxed paper.

Melt chocolate in top of double boiler over hot water. Combine butter and 2 cups hot water in saucepan. Bring to boil. Stir in melted chocolate.

Sift together flour, 4 cups sugar and salt. Pour chocolate mixture into flour mixture all at once. Blend well. Mix in sour cream, vanilla and baking soda.

Add eggs. Turn into prepared pans. Bake at 350°, 30 to 35 minutes or until cake tests done. Remove from oven and cool pans on racks.

Yield: 10 cups batter.
Will make two 10 in. layers

Traditional Wedding Fruitcake
Firm and moist, it's perfect for decorating in the English style. Because of the richness, smaller slices are served. Keep this in mind when figuring servings.

3 cups all-purpose flour
2 tsp. baking soda
1 tsp. baking powder
½ tsp. cloves
½ tsp. nutmeg
½ tsp. cinnamon
½ tsp. salt
1 lb. candied cherries
½ lb. mixed candied fruit
1 jar (8-ounces) candied pineapple
¾ cup dates
1 cup raisins
1½ cups pecans
1½ cups walnuts
½ cup butter
1 cup sugar
2 eggs
½ cup apple or pineapple juice
1½ cups applesauce

Sift and mix flour, baking soda, baking powder, spices and salt.

Cut up fruit and coarsely chop nuts. Mix the fruit and nuts together. Cream butter and sugar. Add eggs and beat well.

Beating until blended after each addition, alternately add dry ingredients and juice to the creamed mixture. Mix in fruit, nuts and applesauce.

Yields 9½ cups of batter.

Fill 3 in. deep pans ⅔ full. This recipe will make one 10 x 3 in. cake.

Turn into a greased pan and bake at 275° about 2½ hours.

Run a knife around sides of pan and let cake set ten minutes in pan. Remove cake and cool thoroughly. It keeps well for two months. It also freezes well, if wrapped tightly.

Baking Hints

- If you like to bake ahead, do so. Your baked cake can be frozen up to three months wrapped in heavy-duty foil.

- Always thaw cake completely before icing. Keep it wrapped to prevent it from drying out. Your cake will still be fresh and easy to ice because it will be firm. It will also have less crumbs.

- Wilton Bake-Even Strips will help prevent crowns from forming on cakes as they bake.

- Packaged, two-layer cake mixes usually yield 4 to 6 cups of batter, but formulas change, so always measure.
Here's a handy guide:
One 2-layer cake mix will make:
two 8 in. round layers, one 10 in. round layer, one 9 x 13 x 2 in. sheet, one mini-tier cake.

- If you're in doubt as to how many cups of batter you need to fill a pan, measure the cups of water it will hold first and use this number as a guide. Then, if you want a cake with high sides, fill the pan ⅔ full of batter. For slightly thinner cake layers, fill ½ full. Never fill cake pans more than ⅔ full. Even if the batter doesn't overflow, the cake will have a heavy texture.

- For 3-in. deep pans, we recommend pound, fruit or pudding-added cake batters. Fill pan half full only.

Buttercream Icing

½ cup solid vegetable shortening
½ cup butter or margarine*
1 tsp. Clear Vanilla Extract
4 cups sifted confectioners sugar
  (approx. 1 lb.)
2 Tbsps. milk**

Cream butter and shortening with electric mixer. Add vanilla. Gradually add sugar, one cup at a time, beating well on medium speed. Scrape sides and bottom of bowl often. When all sugar has been mixed in, icing will appear dry. Add milk and beat at medium speed until light and fluffy. Keep icing covered with a damp cloth until ready to use. For best results, keep icing bowl in refrigerator when not in use. Refrigerated in an airtight container, this icing can be stored 2 weeks. Rewhip before using.
YIELD: 3 cups

*Substitute all-vegetable shortening and ½ teaspoon Wilton Butter Extract for pure white icing and stiffer consistency.

**Add 3-4 Tbsps. light corn syrup per recipe to thin for icing cake.

French Buttercream

⅔ cup sugar
¼ cup flour
¼ tsp. salt
¾ cup milk
1 cup cold butter; cut in several pieces
1 tsp. Clear Vanilla Extract

Place sugar, flour and salt in sauce pan and mix thoroughly; stir in milk. Cook over medium heat and stir constantly until very thick. Remove from heat and pour into a medium mixing bowl. Cool at room temperature. Add ½ cup butter at a time (cut into several pieces) and beat at medium-high speed until smooth. Add vanilla and beat well. Chill icing for a few minutes before decorating. Iced cake must be refrigerated until serving time.
YIELD: 2 cups

Snow-White Buttercream

⅔ cup water
4 Tbsps. Wilton Meringue Powder Mix
12 cups sifted confectioners sugar
  (approximately 3 lbs.)
1¼ cups solid shortening

¾ tsp. salt
½ tsp. almond extract
½ tsp. Clear Vanilla Extract
¼ tsp. Butter Extract

Combine water and meringue powder; whip at high speed until peaks form. Add 4 cups sugar, one cup at a time, beating after each addition at low speed. Alternately add shortening and remainder of sugar. Add salt and flavorings; beat at low speed until smooth.
YIELD: 7 cups.

Note: Recipe may be doubled or cut in half. If cut in half, yield is 2⅔ cups.

Chocolate Buttercream

Add ¾ cup cocoa or three 1 oz. unsweetened chocolate squares, melted, and an additional 1 to 2 Tbsps. milk to recipe. Mix until well blended.

For a unique change of pace, add Wilton Candy Flavors in Rum, Orange or Cherry, in place of vanilla extract.

Stabilized Whipped Cream Icing

1 tsp. unflavored gelatin
4 tsps. cold water
1 cup heavy whipping cream (at least 24
  hours old and very cold)
¼ cup confectioners sugar
½ tsp. Clear Vanilla Extract

Combine gelatin and cold water in small saucepan. Let stand until softened. Place over low heat, stirring constantly just until gelatin dissolves. Remove from heat and cool (gelatin should be cool but still liquid). Whip cream, sugar, and vanilla until slightly thickened. While beating slowly, gradually add gelatin to whipped cream mixture. Whip at high speed until

stiff. YIELD: 2 cups. Cakes iced with whipped cream must be stored in the refrigerator. Hint: Cream may be whipped in a food processor with metal blade. It will have less volume and be velvety smooth.

Cream Cheese Icing

3-8 oz. packages slightly softened
  cream cheese
3 cups sifted confectioners sugar

Beat cream cheese until smooth. Add confectioners sugar and mix thoroughly. Beat at high speed until light and fluffy.
YIELD: 3½ cups

Icing Timesavers

Wilton Creamy White Icing Mix

You'll love its creamy taste, luscious texture and convenience. Ideal for icing smooth and decorating. Just add butter and milk, the shortening's already in the mix. For chocolate icing: Mix icing according to package directions. Stir in 2-oz. melted, unsweetened baking chocolate. If too stiff, add a few drops of milk.

Ready-to-Spread Wilton Decorator's Icing

Ideal for all your decorating needs. Use for frosting, piping borders, flowers, writing and more. Just stir for proper decorating consistency. Tastes delicious, too.

Icing Hints

- When filling layers, use less filling than you usually would. Your dam of icing should also be far enough from edge so filling doesn't flow out and form a bubble in the icing.

- The cake icer tip (789) is an invaluable timesaver in icing wedding tiers.

- You will have less crumbs when icing, if cakes are baked a day in advance.

Specialty Icings

Royal Icing

This smooth, hard-drying icing makes decorations that last. Ideal for making flowers, piping figures, overpiping and decorating cookies. Flowers and decorations made from royal icing will last for months, if stored properly, without softening. Royal icing decorations should be air dried. Allow several hours drying time for large decorations. Make sure bowl and utensils are grease free, since any trace of grease will cause royal icing to break down.

Royal icing dries quickly, so keep icing bowl covered with a damp cloth at all times. Store in airtight container. Rebeat at low speed before using.

Note: Royal icing is edible. Since it dries candy-hard, it is not recommended for icing your cakes. Use only for special effects you want to last.

For piping delicate stringwork, add 1 teaspoon of piping gel or light corn syrup to 1 cup icing.

Royal Meringue Recipe

3 level Tbsps. Wilton Meringue
   Powder Mix
4 cups sifted confectioners sugar
   (approx. 1 lb)
6 Tbsps. water*

Beat all ingredients at low speed for 7 to 10 minutes (10 to 12 minutes at high speed for portable mixer) until icing forms peaks.
YIELD: 3 cups

*When using large countertop mixer or for stiffer icing, use 1 Tbsp. less water.

Royal Egg White Recipe

3 egg whites (room temperature)
4 cups confectioners sugar (approx. 1 lb.)
½ tsp. cream of tartar

Beat all ingredients at high speed for 7 to 10 minutes. Use immediately. Rebeating will not restore texture.
YIELD: 2½ cups

Rolled Fondant

This icing is rolled out and used as a covering for a pound or fruit cake, which is traditionally first covered with a layer of marzipan to seal in flavor and moistness of the cake. It's characteristic of the Australian method of decorating. Traditionally, cakes covered with rolled fondant are decorated with royal icing. Darling and Inspiration are two fabulous examples of rolled fondant cakes.

Rolled Fondant Recipe

1 Tbsp. unflavored gelatin
¼ cup cold water
½ cup Wilton Glucose
1 Tbsp. Wilton Glycerin
2 Tbsp. solid vegetable shortening
2 lbs. confectioners sugar
2-3 drops liquid food color
and flavoring, as desired

Combine gelatin and cold water; let stand until thick. Place gelatin mixture in top of double boiler and heat until dissolved. Add glucose and glycerin; mix well. Stir in shortening and just before completely melted, remove from heat. Mixture should cool until lukewarm.

Next, place 1 lb. confectioners sugar in a bowl and make a well. Pour the lukewarm gelatin mixture into the well and stir with a wooden spoon, mixing in sugar and adding more, a little at a time, until stickiness disappears. Knead in remaining sugar, icing color and flavoring. Knead until the fondant is smooth, pliable and does not stick to your hands. If fondant is too soft, add more sugar; if too stiff, add water (a drop at a time).

Use fondant immediately or store in airtight container in refrigerator. When ready to use, bring to room temperature and knead again until soft. This recipe yields enough to cover a 10 x 3 in. high cake.

To Roll Fondant

Spray work surface and rolling pin with vegetable oil pan spray and dust with a mixture of confectioners sugar and cornstarch. There are two ways to prepare cake for fondant. Coat with piping gel or apricot glaze, then cover with rolled marzipan. Coat again with piping gel or glaze. Add fondant. Or ice cake with buttercream icing, let dry, then cover with rolled fondant.

• Roll out fondant into a circle twice the diameter of the cake you are covering. As you roll, lift and move the fondant to prevent it from sticking to the surface. Gently lift fondant over rolling pin and place over cake.

• Smooth and shape fondant on cake, using palm of hand. If large air bubbles are trapped under fondant, prick with a pin and continue to smooth. Trim excess from base. A fondant-covered cake may be kept up to 2 months, when tightly wrapped and frozen.

Marzipan Recipe

1 cup almond paste
2 unbeaten egg whites
3 cups confectioners sugar
½ teaspoon vanilla or rum flavoring

In bowl, knead almond paste. Add egg white, mix well. Continue kneading as you add flavoring and sugar, 1 cup at a time, until marzipan feels like heavy pie dough.

Color Flow Icing Recipe

Create elegant monograms or a love motif (shown on Romantic Monograms) with this special icing. It dries candy-hard with a satiny-smooth luster.

(Full-Strength for Outlining)
¼ cup water + 1 teaspoon
1 lb. sifted confectioners sugar (4 cups)
2 Tablespoons Wilton Color Flow Icing Mix

In an electric mixer, using grease-free utensils, blend all ingredients on low speed for 5 minutes. If using hand mixer, use high speed. Color Flow icing "crusts" quickly, so keep it covered with a damp cloth while using. Stir in desired icing color. In order to fill in an outlined area, this recipe must be thinned with a ½ teaspoon of water per ¼ cup of icing (just a few drops at a time as you near proper consistency.) Color Flow icing is ready for filling in outlines when a small amount dropped into the mixture takes a full count of ten to disappear. Use grease-free spoon or spatula to stir slowly. Note: Color Flow designs take a long time to dry, so plan to do your Color Flow piece at least 2-3 days in advance.

Color Flow Technique

Tape pattern and waxed paper overlay to your work surface. (The back of a cookie pan makes a good work surface.) For curved decorations, use flower formers. Use full-strength Color Flow icing and tip 2 or 3 to outline the pattern with desired colors. If you're going to use the same color icing to fill in the outlines, let the icing outlines dry a few minutes until they "crust." If you're filling in with icings that differ in colors from the outlines, let outlines dry thoroughly (1-2 hours) before filling in.

Soften icing for filling in outlines as specified in recipe. Don't use a tip for filling in outlines; instead cut a very small opening in end of parchment bag. Begin filling in along the edges of the outline first, squeezing gently and letting the icing flow up to the outline almost by itself. Work quickly, filling in design from the outside edges in and from top to bottom. If you have several outlined sections, fill in one at a time.

If you're filling in a large area, have two half-full parchment bags ready, otherwise icing could "crust" before you finish filling in the pattern.

Note: Since buttercream icing will break down color flow, either position color flow decoration on cake shortly before serving or place a piece of plastic wrap cut to fit on area first.

Pretty Extras That Add So Much

Enhance your cake boards with elegant Tuk 'N Ruffle. Here's how easy it is to surround your cakes with a frilly band of tulle and "lace." To apply: First pipe a ring of royal icing on your foil-covered cake board about 3 in. from the edge. Set the ruffle so the edge of the plastic lines up with the edge of cake board. Press ruffle to secure, then attach cake to cake board.

Lace, ribbons, tulle, flower puffs and fabric leaves are easy to work with and the effects are stunning. Here are just a few suggestions to remember: Nylon lace will not absorb grease so it is the best choice. Be sure to work with waterproof, satiny ribbon for the same reason. Before attaching real trims, let icing crust a bit. Then, if neccessary, dot with icing and secure.

How To Tint Icing

Start with white icing and add the color a little at a time until you achieve the shade you desire. Use a toothpick to add icing color; (use more depending on amount of icing). Hint: Tint a small amount of icing first, then mix in with remainder of white icing. Colors intensify or darken in buttercream icings 1 to 2 hours after mixing, so keep this in mind when you're tinting icing. You can always add extra color to deepen the icing color, but it's difficult to lighten the color once it's tinted. Use White–White Icing Color to make your buttercream icing the purest snow-white!

Always mix enough of any one color icing. If you're going to decorate a cake with pink flowers and borders, color enough icing for both. It's difficult to duplicate an exact shade of any color.

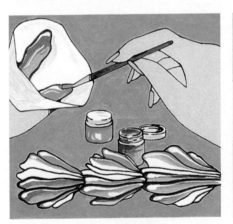

Brush Striping

Striping is a method used to give multiple or deep color effects to icing. To do this, one or more colors are applied to the inside of the parchment paper bag with a brush. Then the bag is filled with white or pastel-colored icing and, as the icing is squeezed past the color, out comes the striped decorations!

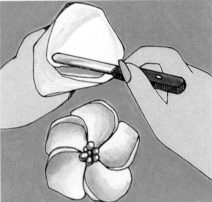

Spatula Striping

Use a spatula to stripe the inside of a decorating bag with Wilton pastel colored icing. Then fill the bag with white icing, or another shade of the same color as the striping, and squeeze out decorations with pastel contrasts.

By following our five-easy-steps icing method, we feel you'll get the results you want.

Leveling

There are two ways to remove the slight crown your baked cake will have. Cool cake for 10 minutes in the pan. Using a serrated knife, with a sawing motion, carefully slice off the raised center. Or unmold cake and allow to cool completely on rack. Invert so that its brown top crust is uppermost and trim away the crust for a flat surface. Our Bake-Even Strips will help prevent crowns from forming on basic shaped wedding cakes.

Filling Layers

Place one cake layer on a cake board or circle atop a cake stand or plate, top side up. Hint: To prevent cake from shifting, smear a few strokes of icing on base surface before positioning cake. Fit bag with coupler and fill with icing. Make a dam by squeezing out a band of icing or filling about ¾ in. high around the top. (If coupler has a slot opening on the side, keep this slot facing downward as you squeeze.) With your spatula, spread icing, jam, pudding or other filling in center. Position top layer with bottom side up.

Icing the Top

Thin your buttercream icing with light corn syrup (approximately 2 teaspoons for each cup). The consistency is correct when your spatula glides over the icing. With large spatula, place mound of icing in center of top and spread across cake, pushing excess down onto sides. Always keep spatula on the icing surface. Touching the cake will mix in crumbs. Hint: To keep your serving base free of icing, place 3 in. wide strips of waxed paper under each side of cake.

Icing the Sides

Cover the sides with excess icing from the top, adding more icing if necessary. Work from top down, forcing any loose crumbs to the cake base. Again, be sure spatula touches only icing. You'll find that an angled spatula is ideal for icing sides.

Smooth Sides & Top

Smooth the side of the cake first, using the edge of the large spatula. Hold the spatula upright against the side of the cake, and slowly spin the stand without lifting the spatula from the cake's surface. Return the excess frosting to the bowl.

Smooth the top of the cake last, again using the edge of the large spatula. Sweep the edge of the spatula from the rim of the cake to its center; then lift it off and remove the excess icing.

Use the same icing procedure as shown here for sheet cakes, heart, oval, square and other shaped cakes with flat surfaces.

A Strong Foundation is Essential.

If the base cake of your design is not on a separator plate, then cover double or triple thicknesses of cardboard or ¼ in. thick piece of fiberboard to support cakes securely.

Wedding Cake Data

The size of the cake is determined by the number of servings needed. Any cake design can be adjusted if the size is too large or too small. Reduce the size by decreasing the size of each tier used. If the design is too small, servings can be increased by using larger tiers or even adding tiers.

For a wedding cake to be attractive and architecturally aesthetic, it must be properly proportioned. A cake can be two, three, four or more tiers. One or more sets of pillars can divide the tiers from one another. Or cakes may simply be stacked together.

A wedding cake tier is usually two layers (or 3 to 4 in. deep). The base tier can be deeper (4 in. or more) than the other tiers. The height of the tiers is important. If tiers are not high enough, the finished cake will be out of proportion. A general rule to follow is a 4 in. difference in tier sizes such as a 6 in. cake atop a 10 in., above a 14 in. tier. But depending on the style and number of servings needed, a 2 in. difference in tier sizes is also acceptable.

The separator set used to separate cake tiers should be one size larger than the cake it supports and one size smaller than the cake on which it sits. To separate a 6 in. and 10 in. tier, 8 in. separator plates should be used.

Pillar height is determined by what, if anything, will be placed between tiers. Popular decorations can include real, silk or icing flowers, ornaments or bells. If nothing is used, we recommend using 3 in. pillars to separate the tiers. If more than one set of pillars is used, all pillars are usually consistent in size.

One cake mix yields 4 to 6 cups of batter. Pans are usually filled ½ to ⅔ full; 3 in. deep pans should be filled only ½ full. Batter amounts on this chart are for pans two-thirds full of batter. Icing amounts are approximate and will vary with consistency, thickness applied and tips used. These amounts allow for top and base borders and a side ruffled border. For large cakes, always check for doneness after they have baked for one hour.

Pan Shape	Size	# Servings 2 Layer	Cups Batter/ 1 Layers 2"	Baking Temps	Baking Time	Approx. Cups Icing to Frost and Decorate
Oval	7¾x5¾"	13	2½	350°	25-30	3
	10¾x7⅞"	30	5½	350°	30-35	4
	13x9¾"	44	8	350°	35-40	5½
	16x12¾"	70	11	325°	45-55	7½
Round	6"	14	2	350°	25-30	3
	8"	25	3	350°	30-35	4
	10"	39	6	350°	35-40	5
	12"	56	7½	350°	35-40	6
	14"	77	10	325°	50-55	7¼
	16"	100	15	325°	55-60	8¾
	18"	127	17½	325°	60-65	10½
Round 3" Deep	8"	15	5	325°	60-65	2¾
	10"	24	8	325°	75-80	4¾
	12"	33	11	325°	75-80	5¾
	14"	45	15	325°	75-80	7
Petal	6"	8	1½	350°	25-30	3½
	9"	20	3½	350°	35-40	6
	12"	38	7	350°	35-40	7¾
	15"	62	12	325°	50-55	11
Hexagon	6"	12	1¾	350°	30-35	2¾
	9"	22	3½	350°	35-40	4¾
	12"	50	6	350°	40-45	5¾
	15"	72	11	325°	40-45	8¾
Heart	6"	11	1½	350°	25	2½
	9"	24	3½	350°	30	4½
	12"	48	8	350°	30	5¾
	15"	76	11½	325°	40	8¾
Square	6"	18	2	350°	25-30	3½
	8"	32	4	350°	35-40	4½
	10"	50	6	350°	35-40	6
	12"	72	10	350°	40-45	7½
	14"	98	13½	350°	45-50	9½
	16"	128	15½	350°	45-50	11
	18"	162	18	350°	50-55	13

Wedding Cake Cutting Guide

This chart shows how to cut popular shaped wedding tiers into pieces approximately 1 in. x 2 in. by two layers high (about 4 in.). Even if you prefer a larger serving size, the order of cutting is still the same.

The first step in cutting is to remove the top tier, and then begin the cutting with the 2nd tier followed by 3rd, 4th and so on. The top tier is usually saved for the first anniversary, so it is not figured into the serving amount.

To cut round tiers, move in two inches from the tier's outer edge; cut a circle and then slice 1 in. pieces within the circle. Now move in another 2 in., cut another circle, slice 1 in. pieces and so on until the tier is completely cut. The center core of each tier and the small top tier can be cut into halves, 4ths, 6ths and 8ths, depending on size.

Cut petal-shaped tiers similar to round tiers as diagram shows.

Cut hexagon tiers similar to round tiers.

To cut heart-shaped tiers, divide the tiers vertically into halves, quarters, sixths or eighths. Within rows, slice one inch pieces of cake.

To cut square tiers, move in 2 in. from the outer edge and cut across. Then slice 1 in. pieces of cake. Now move in another 2 in. and slice again until the entire tier is cut.

To cut oval tiers, move in 2 in. from the outer edge and cut across. Then slice 1 in. pieces of cake. Now move in another 2 in. and slice again until entire tier is cut.

Cutting guides for shapes not shown can be found in other Wilton publications.

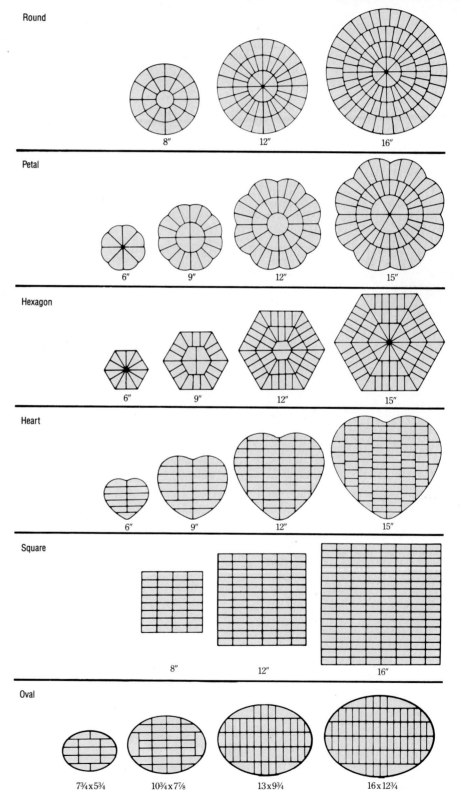

73

Constructing A Tier Cake

To Prepare Cake for Assembly
Place base tier on a sturdy base plate or three or more thicknesses of corrugated cardboard. For heavy cakes, use ¼ in thick fiberboard or plywood. Base can be covered with Fanci-Foil Wrap and trimmed with Tuk-N-Ruffle.

Each tier in your cake must be on a cake circle or board cut to fit. Place a few strokes of icing on boards to secure cake. Fill and ice layers before assembly.

To Dowel Rod Cakes for Pillar & Stacked Construction
Center a cake circle or plate one size smaller than the next tier on base tier and press it gently into icing to imprint an outline. Remove circle.

Dowel Rod

Measure one dowel rod at the cake's lowest point within this circle. Using this dowel rod for measure, cut dowel rods (to fit this tier) the same size using pruning shears. If the next tier is 10-in. or less, push seven ¼-in. dowel rods into cake down to base within circle guide. Generally the larger and more numerous the upper tiers, the more dowels needed. Very large cakes need ½-in. dowels in base tier.

Stacked Construction
This method is often combined with pillar construction. Dowel rod bottom tier. Center a corrugated cake circle, one size smaller than the tier to be added, on top of the base tier. Position the next tier. Repeat procedure for each additional tier. To keep stacked tiers stable, sharpen one end of a dowel rod and push through

Stacked

all tiers and cardboard circles to base of bottom tier. To decorate, start at top and work down.

Pillar Construction

Pillar

Dowel rod tiers. Optional: Snap pegs into separator plates to prevent slipping (never substitute pegs for dowel rods). Position separator plates on supporting tiers, making sure that pillar projections on each tier will line up with pillars below. Mark center backs of cakes. Decorate cakes.

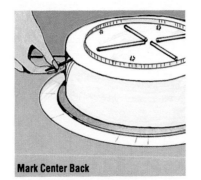
Mark Center Back

• At reception, align pillar projections and assemble cakes on pillars.

Fast & Easy Push-In Leg Construction
Dowel rods are not needed because legs attached to separator plates push right through the tiers down to the plate below.

Mark Where Legs Go

Ice cakes on cake circles. To mark where legs will go, simply center separator plate for tier above (projections down) and gently press onto the tier. Lift plate off. Repeat this procedure for each tier (except top). Position upper tiers on separator plates. Decorate cakes.

Push-In Leg

To assemble: Insert legs into separator plates. Hold tier over base tier, making sure that legs line up with marks. Push straight down until legs touch cake board. Continue adding tiers in this way until cake is assembled.

Spiked Pillars: Like push-in legs, spiked pillows eliminate the need for separator plates on top of tiers. Pillars push into cake to rest on a separator plate or cake circle beneath. When stacking cakes, be sure to double cake circles between cakes to prevent pillars from going through.

Center Column Construction With the Tall Tier Stand

- Each cake involved in construction must be placed on a cake circle or board (cut to fit) with a pre-cut center hole. To do this, trace pan shape on waxed paper. Note: To make positioning easier, place top tier on a slightly larger cake board. Fold pattern into quarters to determine the exact center of each tier. Snip away the point to make a center hole (use cake corer as a guide to size). Trace hole pattern onto boards and cut out.

- Place all tiers on prepared cake boards, attaching with a few strokes of icing. Ice tiers smooth. Using hole pattern, mark centers on all cakes, except top tier. Core out cake centers by pushing the cake corer down to the cake base. Pull out and press cake out of corer.

- Screw a 7¾ in. column to prepare base plate, attaching with the bottom column bolt from underneath the plate. Slip bottom tier over the column to rest on plate. Position columns in all plates except top plate and add cakes.

- The bottom of the plates will not sit level, so to decorate, set plates on the Flower Holder Ring, a pan or bowl. A damp, folded towel or piece of thin foam over the pan will prevent cake from slipping.

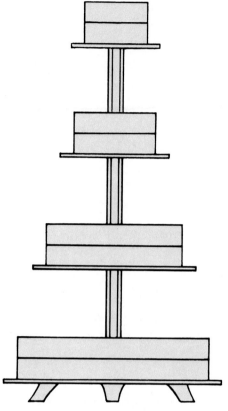

- Since the column cap nut attaches under the top tier, this cake must be positioned after assembling the Tall Tier Stand. Add base borders after assembling the top tier. Or you may place the top tier on a foil-covered cake circle so decorating can be done ahead.

- If using the 4-arm base stand, just attach either a 7¾ in. or 13½ in. column to the center opening with the base nut included.

- To assemble at reception, position plate onto base column section and screw column tight. Continue adding tiers with columns. At top plate, secure columns with cap nut bolt. Position top tier and decorate base.

Hints: To keep balance, cut cakes on the Tall Tier Stand from top tier down.

Using a cake circle under your cake will prevent plates in your from getting scratched during cutting. Be sure to attach to plates with dabs of icing to prevent slipping.

Hints for Assembling & Transporting Tiered Cakes

- Before placing separator plate or cake circle atop another tier, sprinkle a little confectioners sugar or coconut flakes to prevent plate or circle from sticking. Letting icing crust a bit before positioning plate on cake will also prevent sticking.

- When transporting tiers, place cakes on damp towels or carpet foam and drive carefully.

Pillar & Stacked Construction

Push-In Leg Construction

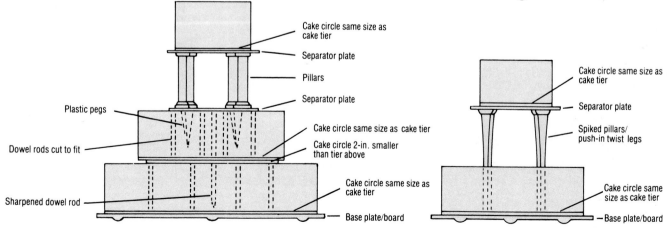

Pillar & Stacked Construction labels:
- Cake circle same size as cake tier
- Separator plate
- Pillars
- Separator plate
- Plastic pegs
- Dowel rods cut to fit
- Cake circle same size as cake tier
- Cake circle 2-in. smaller than tier above
- Sharpened dowel rod
- Cake circle same size as cake tier
- Base plate/board

Push-In Leg Construction labels:
- Cake circle same size as cake tier
- Separator plate
- Spiked pillars/push-in twist legs
- Cake circle same size as cake tier
- Base plate/board

We've included how-to's on some of the more intricate decorating techniques shown on wedding designs in this book. For basic techniques, please refer to the current *Wilton Yearbook of Cake Decorating*.

Drop Strings

Use stiff consistency icing that has been thinned with corn syrup. Many decorators prefer using royal icing for stringwork. With toothpick, mark horizontal intervals in desired widths. Use tip 3. Hold bag at 45° angle to the surface so that end of bag points slightly to the right. Touch tip to first marks and squeeze, holding bag in place momentarily so that icing sticks to surface.

Then pull tip straight out away from surface, without moving tip, allow icing to drop into an arc. Stop pressure as you touch tip to second mark to end string.

Repeat procedure, attaching string to third mark and so on, forming row of drop strings. It's very important to let the string, not your hand, drop to form an arc. Try to keep your drop strings uniform in length and width.

For Double Drop Strings: Start at first mark again, squeeze bag. Let icing drop into a slightly shorter arc than arc in first row. Join end of string to end of corresponding string in first row and repeat procedure.

Always pipe longest drop strings first and add shorter ones. This technique is ideal for cake sides. Practice is important in making drop strings uniform.

Overlapping Drop Strings

With toothpick, dot mark specified intervals on sides of your cake. Touch tip 3 to a mark, allow your string to skip the next mark and attach to the following

one. Return to the mark that was skipped, drop string to the next mark.

Sotas

This intriguing Philippine Method technique is done with tip 1s or 1. It resembles cornelli lace, but the curls, V's and C's of icing are piped very close and overlap. For proper piping consistency, add 1 tsp. of light corn syrup to each cup of buttercream or royal icing used.

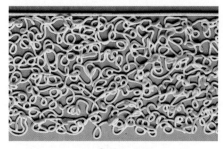

Fleur-De-Lis

Make a shell. Keep bag at 45° angle and starting at the left of this shell, squeeze bag to fan icing into shell base. Then as you relax pressure to form tail, move tip up slightly around to the right, relaxing pressure, forming tail similar to reverse shells. Join to tail of the first shell. Repeat procedure to right side of first shell.

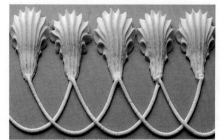

Crown Border

Use tip 32 to make a row of side-by-side upright shells. With tip 4, start at the tail of a shell and drop a string, skip a shell and attach to tail of next shell. Return to tail of shell you skipped, drop a string and skip shell and attach to following shell. Repeat procedure around cakes, keeping the depth of strings even.

Cornelli Lace

With thin icing, use a 90° angle with tip 2 slightly above surface. Pipe a continuous string of icing, curve it up, down and around until area is covered. Stop pressure; pull tip away. Make sure strings never touch or cross.

Zigzag Garlands

Hold bag as for basic zigzag procedure. Allow tip to touch the surface lightly and use light-to-heavy-to-light pressure to form curves of garland. To end, stop pressure, pull tip away. Practice for rhythmic pressure control so garlands are uniform.

Comma, E & S-Motion

Hold bag at 45° angle to surface, finger tips on bag facing you. As you squeeze out icing, move tip down, up to the right and around as if making a comma, e or s. Use a steady, even pressure as you repeat procedure. To end, stop pressure, pull tip away.

Scrolls

Hold bag at 45° angle to surface so that end of bag points to the right. Use tip 3 to draw an inverted "C" center and use circular motion to cover inverted "C." You may overpipe (go over lines) with tip 13 or any small star tip. Use a heavy pressure to feather the scroll, relaxing pressure as you taper end. Add side petals like reverse shells.

These lavish sprays appear on p. 34. Use royal icing to pipe these flowers. To dry: Weight a cake rack at one end and let most of it extend off of counter. As each flower is finished, bend end of wire stem, hook it onto the rack and allow it to dry. When flowers are dry, twist stems together, add ribbons and tulle to form bouquets.

Rose

Pipe center or pistil with tip 5 on a 22-gauge wire. Pipe flower right side up. Twirl a tip 103 ribbon around pistil, keeping tip parallel to pistil. Add 3 closed petals, tiltiing narrow end of tip slightly outward. Surround with 5 open petals, turning narrow end of tip outward at a 45° angle. Dry upside down.

*For instructions to make traditional icing flowers, see the current *Wilton Yearbook of Cake Decorating*.

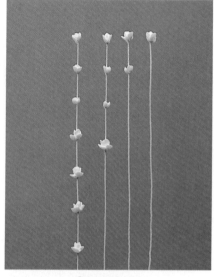

Sampaquita

Pipe a pistil with tip 7. Holding end of wire with pistil down, touch wide end of tip 59 to pistil and pipe 3 closed petals, turning wire like a flower nail. Immediately add 6 outer petals, holding tip at a 45° angle to pistil. Dry upside down on rack.

Rosebud

Pipe small pistil with tip 5. Fill decorating bag with pink icing on one side, white on the other. Hold tip 45 parallel to pistil, wide end about halfway from base, narrow end up. Keeping even pressure, twirl wire, slanting tip out as you finish. Note: This flower is made right-side up. Dry upside down on rack.

Dama De Noche

Pipe pistil with tip 5. Hold wire upside down and touch tip 55 to pistil at 90° angle and squeeze gently. Pull away for a pointed petal. Continue for six-petal flowers. Dry upside down on rack.

Decorating Hints

- Tips from the same basic group that are close in size may be substituted for one another. The effect will be a slightly smaller or larger decoration.

- When using parchment bags, you can place a tip with a smaller opening over the tip you're using and tape it in place. This saves time changing bags and tips when you're using the same color icing.

- To divide tiers, use the Cake Dividing Set. The Wheel Chart makes it easy to mark 2 in. interval on 6 in. to 18 in. diam. cakes. The triangle marker gives precise spacing for stringwork and garlands.

- Stock up on the bags and tips in the sizes you use the most. Your decorating will go faster if several are filled and ready to use. Cover tips securely with convenient Tip Covers. Take along bags of icing in each color used for last minute touch-ups at the reception.

- Any flowers or decorations that are piped on a lily nail or require extensive handling should be made out of royal icing.

- Cake designs specify number of flowers or decorations actually used, so be sure to make extras to allow for breakage.

Wedding Cake Patterns. Trace pattern onto parchment or waxed paper.

Stringwork Patterns for Darling

C (14 in. round)

14 in. top
(¼ of pattern)   Place on fold

Place on fold

Pattern Index

Pattern Name		Cake Name	
Arches A-D	80	Westminster	3.
Butterfly & Petals	80	Fantasia	5(
Heart & Curved Triangles	80	Ruffles & Lace	3(
Stringwork A,B,C	78-79	Darling	8
Scroll	80	Inspiration	1(
Scroll Tops	78	Lady Windemere III	4
Heart &Script Monograms	78-79	Romantic Monograms	
Stairway	79	Sonata	2(
Triangle & Arch	80	Fond Memories	5!

10 in. top

Lady Windemere III
Scroll Patterns

Script Heart

Place on fold

Patterns on grid have to be enlarged. Each square equals ½ inch.

Place on fold

B (center oval)

Place on fold

A (top oval)

Place on fold

Sonata
Stairway Pattern

Script Monograms

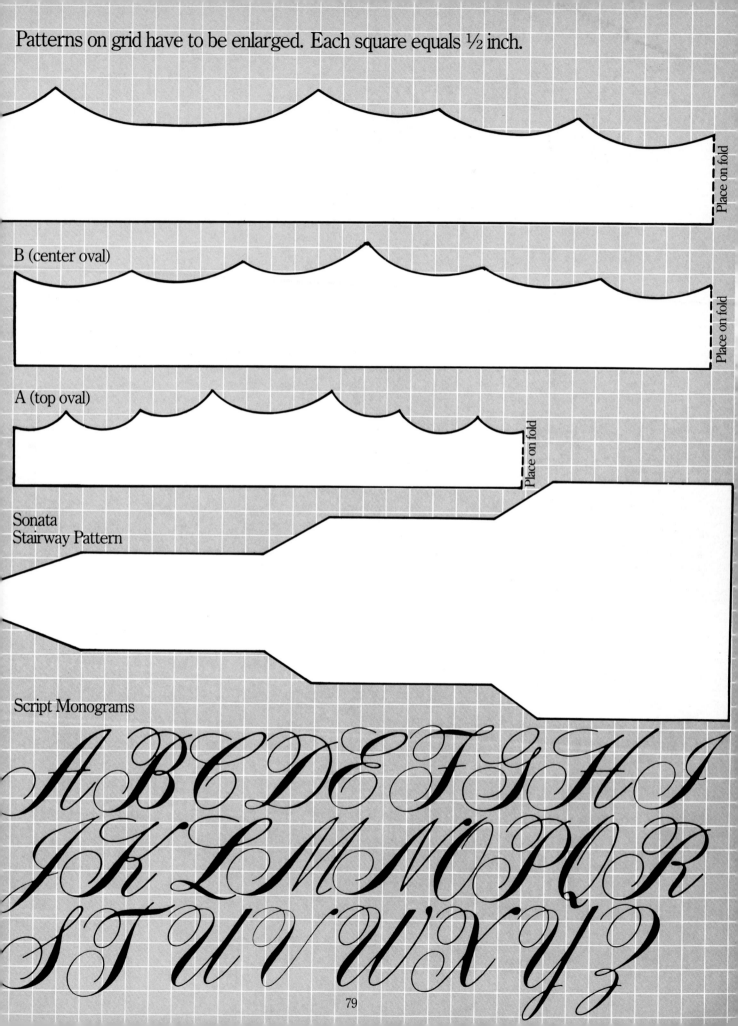

Westminster Arch Patterns

These patterns are actual size

Fond Memories Patterns

B (6″)

Triangle

A1 (6″)

A2 (12″ round satellites)

Place on fold

Arch

D (12″ round)

Inspiration Scroll Pattern

C (On 8″, mark 1″ from corner, 6 points across. On 16″, mark 1¾″ from corner, 11 points across.)

Fantasia Patterns

Butterfly

Petals

Ruffles & Lace Patterns

Curved Triangles

Heart

6″ petal

12″ petal

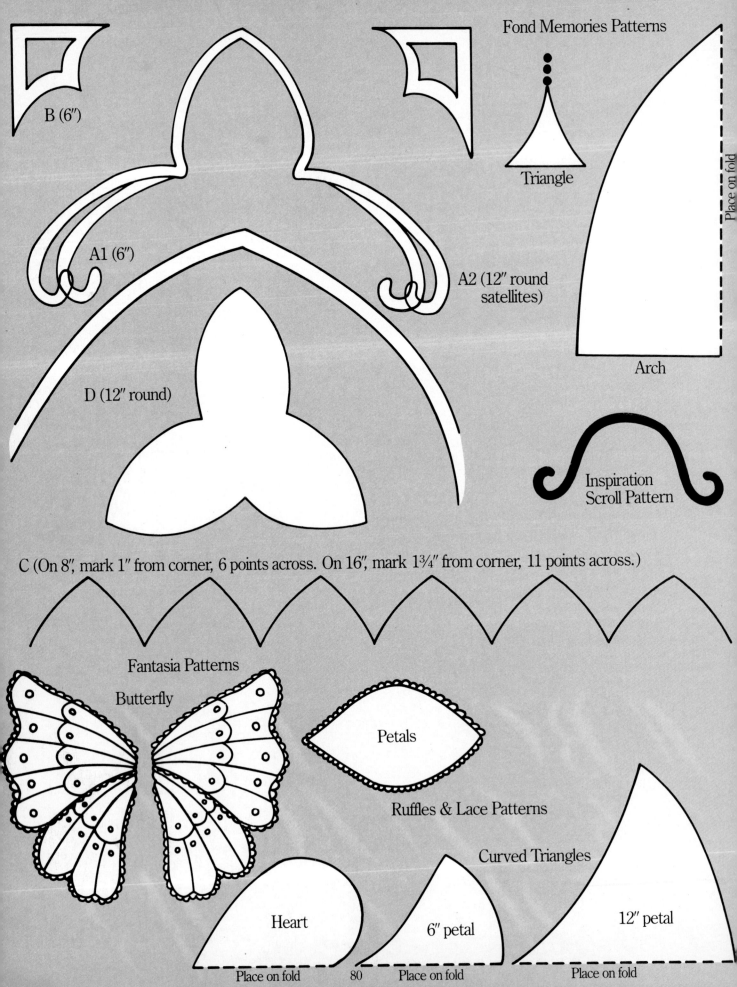